The Art of SERIES

EDITED BY CHARLES BAXTER

The Art of series is a line of books reinvigorating the practice of craft and criticism. Each book is a brief, witty, and useful exploration of fiction, nonfiction, or poetry by a writer impassioned by a singular craft issue. *The Art of* volumes provide a series of sustained examinations of key, but sometimes neglected, aspects of creative writing by some of contemporary literature's finest practitioners.

THE ART OF ATTENTION

A POET'S EYE

Other Books by Donald Revell

POETRY:

A Thief of Strings
Pennyweight Windows: New & Selected Poems
My Mojave
Arcady
There Are Three
Beautiful Shirt
Erasures
New Dark Ages
The Gaza of Winter
From the Abandoned Cities

PROSE:

Invisible Green, Selected Prose

TRANSLATIONS:

A Season in Hell, Arthur Rimbaud
The Self-Dismembered Man: Selected Later Poems
of Guillaume Apollinaire
Alcools, poems of Guillaume Apollinaire

The Art of

ATTENTION

A POET'S EYE

Donald Revell

Graywolf Press

Publication of this volume is made possible in part by a grant provided by the Minnesota State Arts Board, through an appropriation by the Minnesota State Legislature; a grant from the Wells Fargo Foundation Minnesota; and a grant from the National Endowment for the Arts, which believes that a great nation deserves great art. Significant support has also been provided by the Bush Foundation; Target; the McKnight Foundation; and other generous contributions from foundations, corporations, and individuals. To these organizations and individuals we offer our heartfelt thanks.

Clara Ueland and Walt McCarthy are pleased to support the Graywolf Press "Art of" series in honor of Brenda Ueland.

Published by Graywolf Press
250 Third Avenue North, Suite 600
Minneapolis, Minnesota 55401

www.graywolfpress.org

Published in the United States of America

ISBN 978-1-55597-474-9

6 8 10 12 11 9 7 5

Library of Congress Control Number: 2006938268

Series cover design: Scott Sorenson

Cover art: Scott Sorenson

to Norman Finkelstein

HAMM: We do what we can.

CLOV: We shouldn't.

(Samuel Beckett, *Endgame*)

In Arcadia, when I was there, I did not see any hammering stone.

(Henry David Thoreau, *Walden*)

THE ART OF ATTENTION

A POET'S EYE

I

It happens often. I will be reading, a quiet passage concerning something wordless and near—a domestic animal, a flowering plant on a windowsill, an injured bird—and suddenly I find myself still reading the poem but praying too, asking God to watch over the animal, to prosper the flower, to mend the bird. It seems ridiculous, especially when I remember that the poem was written a while ago, sometimes a *very long* while ago, and that in all likelihood the subject of my prayer has long since died. Nevertheless, it's wonderful to be drawn to attend what I am reading so entirely that even its most ephemeral presences are Present to me and matters of concern. Nothing is impossible for such a poem. More than convincing, it is a conviction. More than moving, it is a perpetual, worldly motion. Over my years of reading and writing and teaching, I have hoped to understand just how such conviction, such motion is made to happen. And now I see that poetry is a form of attention, itself the consequence of attention. And, too, I believe that poems are presences, themselves the consequence of vivid presentations, events as may be called, in Dame Julian of Norwich's word, "showings." The attention of reading makes a present case first made, however long ago, by poetry's attention to a kitten or a rose, a crow or a cataclysm. So Ralph Waldo Emerson was right to say, in the *American Scholar*, "There is then creative reading as well as creative writing," and the best poems are irresistible invitations to just such reading because the attention they have paid literally begets a present attention. The creative act is continuous, before, during, and after the poem. An attentive poet delights in this continuity. It is her actual Nature and natural habitat. Let's see.

In "Souvenir d'amitié" (from her 1970 collection *Relearning the Alphabet*), Denise Levertov quietly effects some astonishing conversions.

> Two fading red spots mark on my thighs
> where a flea from the fur of a black, curly, yearning dog
> bit me, casually, and returned into the fur.
>
> Melanie was the dog's name. That afternoon
> she had torn the screen from a door and littered
>   fragments
> of screen everywhere, and of chewed-up paper,
>
> stars, whole constellations of paper, glimmered
> in shadowy floor corners. She had been punished,
>   adequately;
> this was not a first offense. And forgiven,

but sadly: her master knew she would soon discover
other ways to show forth her discontent, her black
    humor.
Meanwhile, standing on hind legs like a human child,

she came to lean her body, her arms and head,
in my lap. I was a friendly stranger. She gave me
a share of her loneliness, her warmth, her flea.

And there I go, after more than thirty years, praying
for Melanie. Just how it is that this long-dead domestic
mischief, this *chienne méchante,* concerns me so, right
now, yet again, is the product and creation of Levertov's
sustained attention. Think of the poem's great canoni-
cal ancestor, John Donne's naughty *carpe diem* masterpiece "The Flea," and delight at how Levertov has, with
the heart in her eyes, converted predatory seduction
into amity, converted the formality of rhetoric into
tenderness and notice. The poem goes past its words,
all the way to Melanie and all the way to now. How?
By beginning to see and then continuing to see. The
poem's trajectory is an eyebeam, not an outline. It is a
visual sequence. The sight of those flea bites conjures a
very present vision of the dog and all the vivid particulars of her afternoon's misadventure. Levertov more
than remembers them; she composes in their presence. By writing very close to these particulars, taking
instruction from their specific gravity ("black, curly,

yearning") and their local enormity ("whole constellations of paper"), she sees farther than any lyric conceit or mere metaphor would allow, all the way over into the loneliness vision lets her share. Thus is amity actually created. Thus does amity still continue in us, though Denise and Melanie are gone. The poem is warm, not with argument, but with attention.

I am speaking of intimacy, which is an occasion of attention. It is the intimacy of poetry that makes our art such a beautiful recourse from the disgrace and manipulations of public speech, of empty rhetoric. A poem that begins to see and then continues seeing is not deceived, nor is it deceptive. It never strays, neither into habit nor abstraction. It is an intimacy in which creative writing and creative reading (the poet reads the world with writing) share together continuous presentations of this world: ones and ones. Such a relation can be tremendous, as Walt Whitman showed:

> Stop this day and night with me and you shall possess
>   the origin of all poems,
> You shall possess the good of the earth and sun,
>   (there are millions of suns left,)
> You shall no longer take things at second or third
>   hand, nor look through the eyes of the dead, nor
>   feed on the spectres in books,

You shall not look through my eyes either, nor take
  things from me,
You shall listen to all sides and filter them from
  your self.

Here, it is Whitman's sense of an ongoing creation ("there are millions of suns left,") that assures us the intimacy of poetry remains original. Attention is pro-creative. Stopping with Walt, we do not stop at all; rather, we fix our senses upon the everlastingly primary text that he, a few lines farther on in "Song of Myself," calls "the procreant urge of the world." The poem of attention is not merely a work in progress; it is a work *of* progress in the most natural sense. Thus is attention an urgent and ecological peace, and what could be more urgent, here and now?

No occasion in modern American poetry can have been more urgent and more complexly intimate with the problem of peace than Ezra Pound's confinement in the gorilla cage at Pisa. Driven to wild error and, as some would have it, to treason by a passion for peace and hatred of war, Pound found himself confined to the very strictest intimacy: a solitude with nothing to read except the ground at his feet and the unfolding text of the sky to which his cell was open, night and day. The progress of such strict intimacy remains to be seen in poems he read and wrote from those texts, *The Pisan Cantos.* Stopped cold in a cage, Pound, almost in spite of himself (he never was a very big fan of Whitman's), found himself in full possession of "the origin of all poems," the continuous present as presented to his eye and to his loneliness, instantly companioned by new intimates. Follow, if you will, the trajectory of this particular eyebeam from the end of "Canto LXXX."

> as the young lizard extends his leopard spots
>   along the grass-blade seeking the green midge
>   half an ant-size
> and the Serpentine will look just the same
> and the gulls be as neat on the pond
> and the sunken garden unchanged
> and God knows what else is left of our London
>   my London, your London
> and if her green elegance
>   remains on this side of my rain ditch
>   puss lizard will lunch on some other T-bone
>
> sunset grand couturier.

So does the poetry of attention indite salvation, restoration, and peace. Pound sees the lizard in its wild enormity stalking prey along a grass-blade. The world is at work, dramatic and wide. Nature is not arrested.

All's well. And this wellness seen up close goes far, all the way to Pound's beloved London where the river, gulls, and garden also go on. His faith restored by sight, Pound continues to see, and the elegant drama of lizard and green fly unfolds along his rain ditch. The pleasures of peace and the gifts of civilization and society are given freely to the open eye by the undetained light of a sunset, the new Pound's (his poem has made him new) "grand couturier." Everywhere in *The Pisan Cantos,* Pound the hysterical aesthete is calmed and renovated by intimates of his eye, as here, in "Canto LXXXIII:"

> mint springs up again
> > in spite of Jones' rodents
> as had the clover by the gorilla cage
> > with a four-leaf
>
> When the mind swings by a grass-blade
> > an ant's forefoot shall save you
> the clover leaf smells and tastes as its flower

In the poetry of attention, the poet comes to his senses. He is saved along the way. Proud mind, which loves to impose itself between appearance and reality (such imposition lies at the core of all bad poems), "swings by a grass-blade" until fact, in the shape of "an ant's forefoot," strides to the rescue. Fact is, faith is, appearance and reality remain tenderly intimate at the origin of poems. Pound knows, having come to his senses: "the clover leaf smells and tastes as its flower." In the attentive occasion that is truth in poetry, what you see is what you get. O taste and see.

As to matters of craft, who among us would wish to be known as "crafty?" The art of poetry is not about the acquisition of wiles or the deployment of strategies. Beginning in the senses, imagination senses farther, senses more. Remember this famous avowal from William Blake's "Vision of the Last Judgement."

> "What," it will be questioned, "when the sun rises
> do you not see a round disk of fire somewhat like a
> guinea?" Oh no, no! I see an innumerable company of
> the heavenly host crying "Holy, holy, holy is the Lord
> God Almighty!" I question not my corporeal or vege-
> tative eye any more than I would question a window
> concerning a sight. I look through it and not with it.

That "disk of fire somewhat like a guinea" condemns craft and all its clever coinage. Blake sees the heavenly host and not something "like" it. His imagination is the capacity of his eye. The art of poetry, then, involves the sustained and sustaining increase of just this capacity.

At sunrise, we may see the sun rising, which is, in fact, a host rejoicing. There you go. Blake sees, and then Blake sees more. The capacity of his eye is the direct consequence of his faith: not faith in a dogma or superstition or simple wish, but faith *in* his eye. The poetry of attention is not metaphysical. It trusts the opened eye to see. By faith, the eye stays open. And so the work of poetry is trust that, by faith, is shown to be no work at all.

Who would wish to be known as "crafty"? Not Blake. And certainly not his luminous contemporary, Goethe. Consider this passage from his *Conversations with Johann Peter Eckermann.*

> ". . . And, finally, how much time is lost in invention, internal arrangement, and combination! for which nobody thanks us, even supposing our work happily accomplished.
>
> "With a *given* material, on the other hand, all goes easier and better.

Time "lost in invention, internal arrangement, and combination"—sounds to me a chillingly accurate assessment of our poetry workshops on any given day. As Blake trusts his eye, Goethe trusts his material. Again the poetry of attention is not metaphysical; it succeeds by faith alone. The opened eye will see, and light will shape the materials given freely to a poet. What need for invention? As it turns out, craft is to poetry what invention is to the imagination—not antithetical, but needless. The eye does not invent the light; there's no need. The mind makes no materials; it doesn't have to. Imagination is the present state of things, and poems rejoice—in particular, in detail—that this is so. Again, the only work is trust, a trust rewarded by ease and by betterment.

The art of poetry is the abolition of doubt. But given human nature, given the vast networks of skeptical re/presentation that human language deploys against the sovereign present state (i.e., against the imagination, Blake's innumerable company), the task of abolition seems strangely formidable. Language purports to fill a need. But what if, as the eye can see, there is no need? Why represent what is surely present? Too, our language is the material of our thoughts. But what if the lavish providence of reality requires no repair, no thought? We must somehow learn to be careless. Though we cannot be unlanguaged we may, perhaps, sometimes by poetry, be unburdened of cares our words presume. Here's a passage from Book III of William Carlos Williams's *Paterson.*

Only one answer: write carelessly so that nothing
that is not green will survive.

The poetry of attention thrives on carelessness, even
as it outspeeds our cares. Greenness is a current even
that must keep current (*courant,* running) to survive.
And so, it seems, to abolish doubt we must study velocities. It's easy, just as Goethe implies. The eye, after
all, is well acquainted with the speed of light.

The eye brings all things near, and the velocity of attention, however great, is instantly intimate. Poetry is a
domestic concern, even on the epic scale. Take, for example, this song from *The Maximus Poems* of Charles
Olson.

Song 3

> This morning of the small snow
> I count the blessings, the leak in the faucet
> which makes of the sink time, the drop
> of the water on water as sweet
> as the Seth Thomas
> in the old kitchen
> my father stood in his drawers to wind (always
> he forgot the 30th day, as I don't want to remember

the rent
      a house these days
so much somebody else's,
especially,
Congoleum's

      Or the plumbing,
that it doesn't work, this I like, have even used paper
   clips
as well as string to hold the ball up And flush it
with my hand
          But that the car doesn't, that no moving
             thing moves
without that song I'd void my ear of, the musickracket
of all ownership . . .
         Holes
in my shoes, that's all right, my fly
gaping, me out
at the elbows, the blessing
              that difficulties are once more

"In the midst of plenty, walk
as close to
bare
     In the face of sweetness,
piss
        In the time of goodness,

go side, go
smashing, beat them, go as
(as near as you can

tear
In the land of plenty, have
nothing to do with it
                              take the way of
the lowest,
including
your legs, go
contrary, go

sing

Here is the surest, sweetest anthem of carelessness I
know. And it begins with, it is begun *by*, a very close
instance of attention: "This morning of the small snow."
It is that word "small," so unusual and so simply absolutely accurate that introduces the tender leisure
speeding this song. The snow is not a concern; it is a
familiar. (How I wish Charles Olson were my weather-
man!) The eye here finds itself among facts as friends,
among blessings. And these are powerful friends indeed. Notice how the fact of the leaky faucet, if you
listen closely, accomplishes a cosmic transformation:
a broken sink becomes time. It doesn't just *keep* it,

like an old Seth Thomas clock; it *becomes* it. And this transformation happens not because of mind and not metaphorically; it happens because Olson listens so closely as to taste and know the "sweet" of the sound: another simple absolute accuracy, an accuracy made by ear not acumen. Small. Sweet. Their sense goes straight to the heart at light speed. And so of course it is no effort (sense is effortless after all) to travel time. Just as the near facts in Pisa sped Pound to his London, so here a leaky faucet magics up a father in his drawers. Everything in this poem is happening very fast, and yet it all seems right and homely because everything is only as it is—a discrete sequence of attentions dearly paid. And speaking of things paid, see how the issue of rent arises, early to dismiss what is later called "the musickracket of all ownership." The poetry of attention proceeds not by acquisition but, rather, by plain accumulation. It doesn't add up; it goes. I see the light, but seeing doesn't make it mine. The broken sink makes magic in this poem, but it isn't Olson's. That's a wonderful thing about renting—repair is never the tenant's problem. Unworried, then, by repair and all such "mind," the poetry of attention is free to delight in what it finds. (To find: *trouver,* or in older French *trobar,* hence "troubador," a poet who does not make but finds.) A broken toilet becomes a marvelous toy, a wacky contraption of improvisational, hand-made fun. And then the song rises to a faster, higher pitch, blessing difficulties, which are not problems because no mind has made them so. Worn-out clothes (a *given* material, just like the sink, as Goethe would approve) provide a gorgeous, giddy Chaplinesque, "Hallelujah, I'm a bum." In the poetry of attention, poems are not problems. (The faculty may return to their homes.) Poems are consequences of circumstance, albeit circumstances of much good consequence—especially as here, where the song literally sends us on our way (not its way), singing. "Song 3" has nothing to do with having, only with going. A sweeter study in velocity I do not know.

In the canon of American velocity, we have an inexhaustible primer in the *Journals* of Henry David Thoreau. Uncrafted, instantaneous, and epical, tossed off in the direction of anyone or of no one and, thus, eternal, their two million words and more instruct us in the rigorous discipline of true carelessness: i.e., in seeing what there is to see and not what we expect or mean to find. Bums and troubadors can have no truck with the intentional fallacy. Everything depends upon attentions innocent of mind and open-eyed. (P.S. the poetry of attention is the "improved infancy" Hart Crane opined—see *White Buildings,* and in particular, "Passage.") In every sighting and incite of his *Journals,* Thoreau proposes to become a poet by being one.

Whatever things I perceive with my entire man—
those let me record—and it will be poetry.

(September 2, 1851)

Attention is a question of entirety, of being wholly present. The poet who fully comes to his senses brings *all* his words, *all* of his cadences when he comes. (He brings his enzymes and his immortal soul as well.) And so a poem has nothing to do with picking and choosing, with the *mot juste* and reflection in tranquillity. It is a plain record of one's entire presence. If the record is faithful—nothing adjusted, nothing exaggerated or nuanced—faith is rewarded: "it *will be* poetry." Why? Because it is. Poems are entireties undisfigured by intent and upheld by perfect attendance. Attention improves our innocence every time. And with time, the poem comes right.

As you *see* so at length will you *say*.

(November 1, 1851)

What shapes the poem? Simple duration. To presence, the poet adds time by adding attention. (Thus is an American masterpiece made of two million offhand words.) To see at length is enough to say, and to say more, see more. Craft elaborates. Attention extends.

On my deathbed, I shall want a longer not a more elaborate life. I shall want an extension, not a revision. And so in the meantime, I take my lesson from Thoreau. I improve my poem by opening my eyes a little wider for a little while longer. Nothing is revised, but vision, as always, changes everything.

> The poet is a man who lives at last by watching his moods.

> *(August 28, 1851)*

To write the poetry of attention is to live "at last," to be free, at last, of those awful ventriloquists, Convention and Memory. Having come to his senses, the poet needs no inner life. He sees his moods spread out before him, a continuous revelation of his present circumstances. There's nothing to elaborate, nothing to work out. Infancy improves with every hour spent in Eden, and attention makes an Eden—i.e., a wholly new heaven and new earth—everywhere, every single time. As Olson said in "Maximus, to Gloucester," it all comes "to the eye and soul/as though it had never/happened before." Why? Because it has never happened before. How do we know that? We've been watching. Our eyes have been open the entire time, i.e. ever since the poem began.

Why did I not use my eyes when I stood on Pisgah?

(January 24, 1852)

The poem is a promised land, and poetry is what happens there. Who would close his eyes to imagine it?

Of all contemporary poets, none has more perfectly visioned with Thoreau's Edenic eye than Ronald Johnson who, in his wild epic, *Ark*, encounters again and again an "Eden, glossolalia of light." With the protraction of sight into saying, Edens are forwarded in real time, the paradise of which is poetry spoken directly to the eye. Where light is sovereign, senses are revelatory, and even prophecy is effortless. The future is apparent to every opened eye. This is the circumstance in which creative writing and creative reading become one and the same. The heliotrope does not imagine the sun, nor does it seek it; it simply, by its nature, finds it out. It is faith incarnate. Not surprisingly, then, a heliotropic poet such as Ronald Johnson finds faithful reading rewarded with poems, such as this, a piece from his *Ark* taken verbatim from Thoreau's *Journals*.

"I look under the lids of time,
   left without asylum
  to gather a new measure

through aisles of ages
art, every stroke of the chisel
enter own flesh and bone

without moving a finger,
turning my very brain
reflected from the grass blades"

(from "Ark 74, Arches VIII")

Johnson finds his poem already written because he reads as he sees, i.e., with open eyes. I know it might seem ridiculous, but then, the world is alive. Think a moment. Enthralled by memory, do we not spend most of our waking life in a dream of *re*cognition, failing to see that everything we see has never been seen before? Enthralled by convention and the *re*presentations of rhetoric, do we not spend most of our reading life *re*reading, failing to see the poem on the page, even our own poem, as something happening Now and so for the first time ever? Revision is sleep. The poetry of attention comes to our senses not as a dream and not as a representation. And Johnson writes it so, gladly professing his poem's measures and his poem's newness to be "gathered," not made. Eyes harvest the light they have not sown. In poetry, seeing is meaning, and Johnson is not ashamed to find it in the deepest sense (as eyes go deeply to the brain) effortless. "Ark 74" was gladly gathered "without moving a finger." The poetry of attention proposes a heroic unoriginality whose entire faith rests in the tireless originality of the real. Eden was already Eden when the gardener arrived. Go ask Adam gladly occupied by paradise, when he was glad. "Ark 74" is likewise literally occupied by Thoreau. When an eye is occupied by light, we call it vision. Johnson avows as much very early in *Ark*, in this passage from "Beam 4":

> The human eye, a sphere of waters and tissue, absorbs an energy that has come ninety-three million miles from another sphere, the sun. The eye may be said to be sun in other form.

"As you *see* so at length you will *say?*" A poem is "said to be sun," Eden spoken directly to the eye. The absorbent eye becomes, Ronald Johnson avers, a sun, a source. Its authority, its authorship if you like, is effortless once it opens. The poetry of attention is absorbed with what is real. Not original *in* itself, it becomes a source of originality simply by its being real. The world is alive. Where is the art? Get real. By which I mean to say the art of poetry is effortless *once it opens.* A poem opens words and the world pours in "as though it had never/happened before."

There is always more to read in more than books, lively as they sometimes are. The world is alive and languaging, though it will not pause to be *re*read or composed. There is no such thing as a still life. The French phrase gives the game away: *nature morte.* Composition is taxidermy. Life presents itself at velocities beyond representation, but quick attentions can quicken our poems, and then oh how prolific all presences become. See here in a poem from Ronald Johnson's 1967 collection *The Book of the Green Man.* Nothing that is not green will survive—

What the Leaf Told Me

Today I saw the word written on the poplar leaves.

It was 'dazzle'. The dazzle of the poplars.

As a leaf startles out

from an undifferentiated mass of foliage,
so the word did from a leaf—

A Mirage Of The Delicate Polyglot
inventing itself as cipher. But this, in shifts &
    gyrations,
grew in brightness, so bright

the massy poplars soon outshone the sun . . .

'My light—my dews—my breezes—my bloom.'
   Reflections

In A Wren's Eye.

This is not creative writing. This is poetry. Johnson pays attention to a leaf and sees what is written there. (America's greatest symphonist, Charles Ives, once declared "American music is already written," rhyming with a most sensible passage in *Walden:* "I awoke to an answered question.") Johnson quickens to the language of a leaf, and his reward is dazzling. And "dazzle" gives the poem all of form and content it can hold, and then some. This is what Goethe meant by *"given* material." Matters of form and content and all such workshop mumbo jumbo disappear in the sovereign dazzlement of a material world, once the bright activity of its material shines. There simply isn't, as Charles Ives knew, any work to do. The poetry just keeps happening. Prolific light unfolds the sun into the shape of a leaf. It's startling, and it writes the poem, which is only one of the leaf's numerous languages: "A Mirage Of The Delicate Polyglot." And this is a new poem in mid-poem or after the first one. Johnson is listening so quickly he can hear the world interrupting itself, reinventing itself. See, he isn't composing. There is no leisure for composition when things are happening so fast. (They are *always* happening so fast.) The brightness grows until each poplar, each mass of particular dazzling leaves (they dazzle *with* their particularity, that's the point that puts the world so far ahead of simile) is a sun and more than a sun unto itself. (Remember Whitman—"there are millions of suns left.") Separateness—a leaf—and mass—"the massy poplars"—are seen as coevals, co-eternal. Turns out there are more eternities than one. That's more revelation than eleven lines can hold. Happily, Johnson has no wish to hold it. Where the eye is rapt, each word is a rapture. What's happening? The words cannot contain themselves, much less the world. They are suns, not jars of lightning bugs, after all. The poem cannot contain the poetry. Sunlight is faster than the sun itself, and so it shines. Here, poetry is faster than the poem. *"What the Leaf Told Me"* breaks off at the title of a new poem it is not fast or rapt enough to read, not now, not yet: "In A Wren's Eye." Blinded in the white space, Johnson has faith in another eye to come and further transformations.

It's good to know his faith was amply kept and abundantly rewarded, time and again, poem by poem. Johnson's books show supernumerous traces of light active in the world. It's a rapture to read them. His eye was rapt until the end. In his last years, working as a handyman and gardener in Topeka, he wrote a collection published posthumously as *The Shrubberies*. Near its center is a poem of a single line, untitled:

Yes Heaven/being/garden

The opened eye consents to Heaven. Heaven is a fact. Facts are gardens. Eden is already forever Eden when the attentive poet comes.

We have come to the point of ecstasy, a poetic of delight delightful in itself, but difficult, perhaps even problematic, to sustain. I do not want to proprose the poetry of attention as a glossolalia, a speaking in tongues only. We live in several dimensions at least, and they are not *all* vertical. In poems, we address ourselves severally (remember Denise and Melanie) over the course of a writing life, not always to Eden or everlastingness alone. The poetry of attention sometimes leads to raptures, as we have seen. But more importantly, more fundamentally, its ways and its means are those of peace—peace even at the level of the syllable; peace even at the center of the eye. There comes a point when a poet's faith in her material *as given* constitutes a truly material Faith. The eye, accepting the reality of what it sees (key to the poetry of attention is *accep-*

tance) concedes a certain sovereignty, and so attention becomes a form of obedience informed and/or inspired by faith. Aggression is always predicated on fantasy; it is the imagination's preemptive strike upon sovereign facts whose reality it refuses to concede, much less to worship. To see the sovereignty of what is seen is, quietly, really to worship. And to articulate such worship in a poem Wages Peace. So quiet a poem, then, as William Carlos Williams's "The Red Wheelbarrow" *must* be, among so many other things, a prayer and a call for peace.

> so much depends
> upon
>
> a red wheel
> barrow
>
> glazed with rain
> water
>
> beside the white
> chickens.

As in any authentic prayer, the very first utterance— "so much depends"—freely concedes authority and sovereignty. What follows is the piety of the poet's eye, keeping faith with each and every particular it sees. (Spare as he seems, Williams sounds a principle of inclusiveness, not of selection—how else explain those ultimate chickens? Editors, take note.) And faith is kept in sequence. (Williams, unlike so many poets, is glad that Time is real.) "The Red Wheelbarrow" never totalizes, never seizes an advantage via aggressive metaphor or mind. The effect is peace. All's well. All's here. The circumstance of dependency is delightful *in its materials:* redness and rain, barrow and wheel. It is pleasing to believe that the world is real, and the pleasure is peace.

In the poetry of attention we therefore find a pious materialism. Sad and strange that these two notions— piety and materialism—should be so generally proposed (and opposed) as antitheses. Their separation banishes the eye to a wilderness of mirrors. It banishes poetry to a metaphysical preschool. It compels aggression, setting sanctity loose upon unimproved matters of fact, constructing God knows how many golf courses, both real and metaphorical, as it goes. (I fly each week of the academic year from my home in Arden, Nevada, to my job at the University of Utah, and I cannot tell you how many times I have overheard some passenger propose to "improve" the glorious spaces of Zion National Park or the Wasatch Mountains with a golf course.) It's un-American. Wasn't the very first chapter of *Walden* called "Economy" and wasn't Thoreau's economy expressed as faith in the worlding *(natur naturans)* of the world?

> I think that we may safely trust a good deal more than we do. We may waive just so much care of ourselves as we honestly bestow elsewhere. Nature is as well adapted to our weakness as to our strength. The incessant anxiety and strain of some is a well nigh incurable form of disease. We are made to exaggerate the importance of what work we do; and yet how much is not done by us!

"*Thine* is the kingdom [italics mine]." This rhymes with "The Red Wheelbarrow," a poem that entrusts its form and literally every one of its words not primarily to what the poet does, but to what is already accomplished, e.g., by redness and by rain. The ongoing accomplishment, the work of the world worlding, of course, is peace. The poetry of attention trusts the given, believing trust prolongs, even to the point of profusion, this true peace.

In accepting a limited role, a limited originality ("humility is endless"—T. S. Eliot, "East Coker"), the poet of attention makes a liberating peace with what, in fact, eventually enlarges his vision beyond imagining. This is *kenosis,* a notion at work in our words as far back as Paul's letter to the Philippians.

> Let this mind be in you, which was also in Christ Jesus:
> Who, being in the form of God, thought it not robbery to be equal with God:
> But made himself of no reputation, and took upon him the form of a servant, and was made in the likeness of men:
> And being found in fashion as a man, he humbled himself, and became obedient unto death, even the death of the cross.
> Wherefore God also hath highly exalted him, and given him a name which is above every name . . .
>
> *(Philippians 2: 5–9)*

The divine, however it is we understand such an incomprehensible entity, humbles itself, empties itself (*kenosis* means "to empty") into the world as worldling: in this instance, a human being called Jesus who lived and died. Where was the material of the cosmos before there was a cosmos? It can only have been identical with whatever we trust as divine: primary matter, primary motion. (Motive we must leave to theologians and philosophers.) And where is this divinity now?

Profusing its peace through all the matter moving in the world. So it is simply natural that plain attention is a piety and that the unaggressive articulation of attention in poems may be a form of prayer, an instance of worship, a forwarding of peace. Conceding the creative to creation, by coming literally to his senses, the poet accepts a limited role in poetry comparable to that of God when he, she, or they emptied an original divinity into the ongoing creation of the world. (I reckon this is what Jack Spicer meant by his famous injunction in "Imaginary Elegies": "Poet be like God.") Not too shabby for a limitation, yes?

Things are getting rapturous again, and just when I meant to be speaking of quietness and peace. But as it turns out, a quiet sense inclines to be rapt, just as peace inclines toward rapture. In our own time, no one has written more gently and more radically of these inclinations than John Cage. (I love that his middle name was "Milton"!) In the 1961 collection *Silence,* Cage describes the quiet action of the attentions as a force for change.

> Wherever we are, what we hear is mostly noise.
> When we ignore it, it disturbs us. When we listen to
> it, we find it fascinating.
>
> (from *"The Future of Music: Credo"*)

Listening does not make the music. It does, however, put us in glad relationship to music already playing: the music of the world. A musician is inclined to listen; and when he listens, the sounds are music. So does the attentive poet's inclination lead to poems— to a red wheel barrow, for example, and to all the cosmos of relations (white chickens, rain water) that attention enters in. The musician orients us to listen. The poet orients us to read. The artist is not in control of the music or the poetry, but her attentive presence so inclines us that we hear and read anew.

> The mind, though stripped of its right to control, is still present. What does it do, having nothing to do?

> *(from "Composition as Process")*

Kenosis again. The acceptance of limits joins us to limitlessness. As a subject, the wheel barrow only goes so far. But as an object, an object of attention, it is inexhaustible. Its relations are limitless. The eye can trace a line from the barrow to eternity. How? By having nothing to do with control or with the various aggressive means by which control is always, however fantastically, proposed. One cannot show you a wheel barrow by saying "Look at me." One cannot show the music of the earth by shouting. What do we do having nothing to do? Be present. Commend presence. Keep our peace. Incline our senses as ourselves toward those masterworks—the noise becoming music, the rain becoming a glaze—always already underway.

The inexhaustible refreshment of the opened eye brings immensities near and shows in the near world energies and patterns reaching immeasurably far. In the poetry of attention, consciousness is not confinement; words are not settlements; and the limits of the line go quietly beyond control into the peace of the white space. Confined to a wheelchair from childhood until his death in 1996, Larry Eigner wrote more than forty books of poetry, beginning with the 1953 collection *From the Sustaining Air.* In each book, the eye attests to immensities light travels on its behalf. And all are near, all active in the familiar world. Eigner sees that there is nothing strange in the uncanny, and that revelation is never out of the ordinary in a cosmos always only just now coming into view. A poem proceeds, he wrote, from an "initiation of attention," and then is taken up into the new work of the day. The stillness of the poet is unstilled by sight, but not disturbed. Attention is transport. Here's a piece from 1977:

[trees green   the quiet sun]

trees green   the quiet sun

shed metal truck in the next street
passing the white house you listen
onwards

you heard

the dog

through   per
formed circles

the roads near the beach

rectangular

rough lines of the woods

tall growth   echoing

local water

Eigner entrusts the work of poetry to white space more than most. And notice here how the space does not perforate or inundate the poem, but, rather, embraces it, emboldening each phrase with the leisure to become what each in fact is: tremendous. Eigner neither asserts nor insists. He is a witness to peace at its wild work. He is not reticent. He is patient, and his patience is amazed. All elements are active elementally here. "Trees green" turns "green" into a verb. The sun's quiet makes the next street audible and then visible as listening becomes a form, like a truck, of transport too: "you listen/onwards." Attention unconfines the ear and then the eye and then everything while the poem goes even more wildly into white space. But the wild work is peace. Antitheses are not antagonists and so not antithetical at all: circles jibe with the rectangular; roads bring the woods and ocean close; the far verticals of the trees echo nearly in horizontal "local water." With a very few words and no rhetoric at all, no persuasion, Eigner finds a new threshold in every line. And so do we. And so we cross. The poet does not mean to move. Rather, he is moved to the meaning of what there is to see. The art of poetry is indeed an "initiation of attention" to coherences art could not compose. Compared to the facts, arguments are incoherent, dependent, like Republicans, on discord. This is most important.

Eigner is not passive here; he is unaggressive. The activated eye (light is stimulus after all) accepts each thing in its particularity and in the order of its arrival. This is a method, a technique if you will, practical as well as ideal. Imposing no order, the poet finds one, the coherence already there *in place*. As the poem proves, that place is moving. Eigner's is an activist patience, a stillness accelerated by "the quiet sun." And there I go, getting rapturous again.

I know that what I call the poetry of attention might well be better thought of as "passages" of attention. Poets like Larry Eigner and Ronald Johnson are rare, and the quiet ecstasy they somehow sustain is almost always, at best, intermittent in anyone's work, and necessarily so. Paradise is not a permanent address, at least not yet. There is poetry outside of Eden too. But to the extent that the peace of pure attention can be prolonged or even plainly advocated in a poem, to just that extent does the poem *wage* peace, and to just that extent does the poem gain access to the clarity, the virtue, and the immediacy (mediation is aggression) of that peace. In such moments, it is as if the representational distortions of language themselves have disappeared, leaving poet, poem, and reader together in a perfect transparency, a perfect world (my subtext obviously is that the world *is* perfect) in which, as Wallace Stevens avowed, "being there together is enough" ("Final Soliloquy of the Interior Paramour"). Hart Crane was promised an improved, not a perfected infancy, yet what a peril it is to lose sight (of course I mean this literally) of the infant's perfect eye. Without innocence, experience can only repeat itself. Isn't that Blake's great and liberating theme? Without the innocent eye (*innocere*, to do no harm), a poem's attentions can only dissipate into mists of metaphor or into a machine-shop of argument, that dark Satanic mill. Thomas Traherne, the sublime seventeenth-century precursor of Ronald Johnson (Johnson's selected poetry, *To Do As Adam Did*, takes its title from a passage of Traherne) makes the point purely:

A simple Light from all Contagion free,
A Beam that's purely Spiritual, an Ey
That's altogether Virgin, Things doth see
    Ev'n like unto the Deity:
That is, it shineth in an hevenly Sence,
And round about (unmov'd) its Light dispence.

The visiv Rays are Beams of Light indeed,
Refined, subtil, piercing, quick and pure;
And as they do the sprightly Winds exceed,

Are worthy longer to endure:
They far out-shoot the Reach of Grosser Air,
Which with such Excellence may not compare.

But being once debas'd, they soon becom
Less activ than they were before; and then
After distracting Objects out they run,
    Which make us wretched Men.
A simple Infant's Ey is such a Treasure
That when 'tis lost, w' enjoy no reall Pleasure.

(from "An Infant-Ey")

There you have it. The innocent eye sees "Ev'n like unto the Deity," conforming to Spicer's lovely imperative, "Poet be like God." The innocent eye "shineth in an hevenly Sence," i.e., becomes a source of light itself, confirming Johnson's proposal that "the eye may be said to be sun in other form." Every poem needs its portion of the unprecedented, and only the innocent eye, God-like and luminous, brings the unprecedented into view. Innocence is technique and method of the unmethodical eye. The passages of *its* attention will be the most active ones—activating the senses and actuating objects—in *any* given poem. And without such passages, without at least one such, the poem loses sight of the "reall Pleasure" of poetry, which is the pleasure of peace, the pleasure of the immediate present, un-mediated by mind. I think of a passage from the Gospel of St. Luke—"Verily I say unto you, Whosoever shall not receive the kingdom of God as a little child shall in no wise enter therein" (Luke 18:17). A passage of inno-cent attentions may prove a Paradise indeed.

I mean to close this chapter as I began, close-reading a poem by Levertov. This seems right and best to me, as she was the very first contemporary poet whose books I read and sometimes even purchased in the heav-enly Eighth Street Bookshop, gone now, in Greenwich Village circa 1970. Levertov opened my eyes, you might well say, to lines of verse becoming passages of Edenic attention. She was very much of a company with Blake and Traherne, Williams and Johnson; indeed, it was she who, during her time as an editor at Norton, first brought the work of Ronald Johnson to broad national attention. In later years, we corresponded a little, and I remember how quietly amazed I was that her letters and postcards always arrived just when I needed their cautions and encouragement the most. She kept my eyes open. Once, she enclosed the draft of a new poem with a letter, a draft written on a city bus on a blank page torn from a book of my own work, *Beautiful Shirt.* In a very few lines (in a poem whose title I will *not* men-tion, thank you very much, although I will say it was collected in *Sands of the Well*) she'd managed to find the very heart of my intention, and also its refractory peril. She helped me. I'm sad to know that the postman will bring no more of her letters. Still, her books continue to deliver sweet correction, refreshment, and lots of good news. In her last collection, published posthumously under the title *This Great Unknowing*, there's a poem called "First Love." Here, one instance of exquisitely innocent attention proves passage enough to cross the span of a lifetime and to close the distance between Heaven and earth.

It was a flower.

There had been,
before I could even speak,
another infant, girl or boy unknown,
who drew me—I had
an obscure desire to become
connected in some way to this other,
even to *be* what I faltered after, falling
to hands and knees, crawling
a foot or two, clambering
up to follow further until
arms swooped down to bear me away.
But that one left no face, had exchanged
no gaze with me.

This flower:
                    suddenly
there was *Before I saw it,* the vague
past, and *Now.* Forever. Nearby
was the sandy sweep of the Roman Road,
and where we sat the grass
was thin. From a bare patch
of that poor soil, solitary,
sprang the flower, face upturned,
looking completely, openly
into my eyes.
                    I was barely
old enough to ask and repeat its name.

'Convolvulus,' said my mother.
Pale shell-pink, a chalice
no wider across than a silver sixpence.

It looked at me, I looked
back, delight
filled me as if
I, not the flower,
were a flower and were brimful of rain.
And there was endlessness.
Perhaps through a lifetime what I've desired
has always been to return
to that endless giving and receiving, the wholeness

of that attention,

that once-in-a-lifetime

secret communion.

Not a secret anymore, but always. Here, hushed retrospect is kindled by a single rapture into blaze. Even
one attention is numberless. See how nothing what-
soever is withheld or delayed between the poem's title
and its very first line. What was First Love? A flower.
Levertov has no interest at all in the false privilege or
rhetorical advantages of memory. She speeds to her
senses, not even waiting for language, but beginning in
a place where she has no words at all, "before I could
even speak." In such a place, connections and contact
are not about control but about transformation. The
child means to *"be,"* not merely to touch. Soon, eventually (attention makes events of every object) the object
of First Love is simply there—not prepared, but present. And it proves to be an eternal present tense: *"Now.
Forever."* From this point forward, the child's rapture
shines a light. Attention thrives. It notes the powerful
plain fact of antiquity's coeval sweep with sand and soil
at the Roman Road. It notes the thinness of the grass.
(Oh how Levertov's "thin" rhymes with Olson's "small"
as in "This morning of the small snow." Only an innocent eye sees so.) And only then is the flower named,
and not by the poet. Knowledge comes to the senses

from outside, first and always; it is not an advantage; it is Mother and world. And knowledge is not the end of it. (Poets, take note: knowledge is not the end of it!) Delight speeds on. Transformation transpires in a gaze: "It looked at me, I looked/back." Heaven is established on an eyebeam—*"And there was endlessness."* What Levertov comes to see as the "wholeness" of one attention is indeed just that: whole, an ongoing entirety. There is not a whisper of regret, but, rather, anticipation at the end. An opened eye anticipates the light. Once in a lifetime? Once is a lifetime, and longer, being, as the line avers, an endlessness. As ever, Levertov is just too good to let her poem outshine a flower, to take credit for a Heaven freely given from a shell-pink chalice. In conclusion, I add only my opening words. It happens often.

Scholium #1—On Piety

The art of poetry, as I hope to understand it, is not an advantage but, rather, a better access to energies and virtues already prolific everywhere I turn. This is where piety comes in. Think, for example, of the distance we travel as a species and as individual women and men when we leave behind us the wily Odysseus and move instead in the direction of that less clamorous hero, pious Aeneas. By wiles, Odysseus wades through rivers of blood to reclaim his sovereignty. By piety, Aeneas finds the shade of his father in the Groves of Blessedness, there to learn the duties of his soul to itself and to futurity. By cunning, Odysseus, the sole survivor of his journeys, re-establishes himself. By piety, Aeneas brings his disestablished Trojan people home to new shores and a continuing city. Here, in the beautiful Allen Mandelbaum translation of *The Aeneid*, is what Anchises speaks when he sees his son approaching across the green valley floor of Elysium:

> "And have you come at last, and has the pious
> love that your father waited for defeated
> the difficulty of the journey? . . ."

> *(Book VI, 908–910)*

Piety is heavenly transportation. It gets from here to there. Wiles can only close a circle, ending where they began and more alone. I suppose you've been to as many poetry readings as I have, and I'm sure you remember quite a few at which there came a moment when nearly everyone in the crowd said "ooooh" as though in unison because the poet on the podium had, by exquisite guile, brought them all to the same instant of admiration for his sensibility and craft. Ladies and gentlemen, I give you the Odyssean poet, the shining isolate center of a circle he has made. The energy flows from the podium (or page) and then back. The audience (or reader) remains a circumference in the dark. I live in Las Vegas; I see the magic shows all the time. And then there are, I hope, those *other* poetry readings where each is at a different moment moved to a new place entirely his own. The event has no fixed center or climax, but a sense of motion, uncertain but very good and welcome, entirely prevails. A circle whose center is everywhere and whose circumference is nowhere, as the saying goes. And when I remember the poets of those evenings (John Ashbery, for example, or Denise Levertov, or James Schuyler, or Jean Valentine) what I remember is something much more like love than like admiration. What I remember is an active sense of piety, moving in a meadow. Friends, the Aenean poet disappears into numberless continuities he does not own. His vision leads to visions and not back upon itself. The pious eye is reliable transportation. It is also, as Virgil knew, a countless posterity.

And William Wordsworth knew it too, putting the case in its purest state:

> My heart leaps up when I behold
>   A rainbow in the sky:
> So was it when my life began;
> So is it now I am a man;
> So be it when I shall grow old,
>   Or let me die!
> The Child is father of the Man;
> And I could wish my days to be
> Bound each to each by natural piety.

A good wish and one of the most guileless poems in the language. Never be embarrassed by purity; it goes far. Piety is simply a matter of life and death, sole guarantor of good posterity: active innocence; the Child father, not the Father's child. And whence does it arise? When the pure heart leaps its leap of faith into the eye. Luke 18:17, *passim.*

Scholium #2—On Nonaggression

In "Maximus, to himself," Charles Olson offers a beautiful and humble assessment of his gifts as a poet—an altogether pious task at the outset of what would become American Postmodernism's signature epic. Midway through the poem, we find this passage:

> I have made dialogues,
> have discussed ancient texts,
> have thrown what light I could, offered
> what pleasures
> doceat allows
>
> But the known?
> This, I have had to be given,
> a life, love, and from one man
> the world.

The work of peace in poetry begins at the limits of making, where efforts are displaced by amazement and by attachment and by the gratitudes in which every sense is refreshed by what it finds: i.e., the world. The "one man" to whom Olson refers so gratefully is Alfred North Whitehead. In *Process and Reality* (1929), Whitehead details a "Philosophy of Organism" keyed to process as it carries all material, sunlight and consciousness included, forward to the objective immortality of the Real. Because the world works, we are already always at peace, if only we consent to what our senses show: a sovereign process underway before and after our words. And so the work of peace in poetry continues as an ongoing consent, foregoing the aggressions of direction and control. The world is "given." What is there to win? Whitehead puts it beautifully:

> In sense-perception we have passed the Rubicon, dividing direct perception from the higher forms of mentality, which play with error and thus found intellectual empires.

> *(from* Process and Reality, *173)*

The poetry of attention—sustained attention is sustained consent—has neither need nor wish to "play with error." All's given, and the alternative to everything is only a nothing, an aggressive fantasy of "intellectual empire," a crafted Hell in Heaven's despite. The higher mentality is the world itself. What have we been thinking?

Scholium #3—"Who made the eyes but I?"

I am forever urging my friends and students to believe that the poetry of attention is always and only love poetry. Not, of course in the *carpe diem* sense—what could be *less* convincing to a beloved than Andrew Marvell's "To His Coy Mistress," a poem in which the speaker falls hopelessly in love with his own conceits, entirely forgetting his more tender purpose. Not surprising, then, that by the end of that most shopworn of anthology pieces, lovemaking comes down to a passage of "rough strife." Metaphysics is always aggressive. And by love poetry neither do I mean the lover's complaint, the sort of occasion that prompts John Donne to deploy his clever flea to prove chastity a "sacrilege" and lovemaking a trivial bit of bloodshed. Wit is always impious *and* aggressive, too. Peace and piety comprise the actual circumstance of love poetry, and no argument. Where effort yields to inarguable attachment—eyebeam and heartstring—love is all. George Herbert knew.

Love (III)

Love bade me welcome: yet my soul drew back,
      Guilty of dust and sin.

But quick-eyed Love, observing me grow slack
            From my first entrance in,
Drew nearer to me, sweetly questioning
            If I lacked anything.

"A guest," I answered, "worthy to be here":
            Love said, "You shall be he."
"I, the unkind, ungrateful? Ah, my dear,
            I cannot look on thee."
Love took my hand, and smiling did reply,
            "Who made the eyes but I?"

"Truth, Lord; but I have marred them; let my shame
            Go where it doth deserve."
"And know you not," says Love, "who bore the
    blame?"
            "My dear, then I will serve."
"You must sit down," says Love, "and taste my meat."
            So I did sit and eat.

Love lives in the eye; it is quick there. It furthers the
eye in the direction of its inarguable innocence. Heaven
knows, George Herbert tries to argue—"I cannot look
on thee"—but love is just too quick and, by the way,
all-powerful. "Who made the eyes but I?" Effort ends

because it was mistaken from the first and from before the first, all in vain because, all protest not withstanding, effort is vanity. This isn't a workshop. "You must sit down." Light feasts the eye. Love feasts the poet. Anywhere you look, it's a love poem.

II

All this long eve, so balmy and serene,
Have I been gazing on the western sky,
    And its peculiar tint of yellow green:
And still I gaze—and with how blank an eye!
And those thin clouds above, in flakes and bars,
That give away their motion to the stars;
Those stars, that glide behind them or between,
Now sparkling, now bedimmed, but always seen:
Yon crescent Moon, as fixed as if it grew
In its own cloudless, starless lake of blue;
I see them all so excellently fair,
I see, not feel, how beautiful they are!

(from "Dejection: An Ode,"
Samuel Taylor Coleridge)

Nous n'aimons pas assez la joie
De voir les belles choses neuves
[We have never loved the joy of seeing
New things with adequate intensity]

(from "La Victoire," Guillaume Apollinaire,
translation mine)

Most of the time, what good is a poet to himself? I mean, what is there to do outside the transformative ecstasy of perfect attentions? Is there only, as T. S. Eliot supposed in his "Burnt Norton," "Ridiculous . . . waste sad time/Stretching before and after"? Do we mostly stop and merely stay at the threshold of miracles already receding, miracles such as the one of which James Wright's "A Blessing" just falls, *almost* blissfully, short?

> . . . if I stepped out of my body I would break
> Into blossom.

So much of life, so much of our writing lives, is prelude and aftermath, anxiety and exhaustion. (As I get older, I more and more suspect that weariness and fretfulness are one and the same.) When Coleridge, with such awful accuracy, defines dejection as sight continuing in Vision's absence, as the drone of perception deprived of contact ("I see, not feel, how beautiful they are!"), I wonder and worry with him—just where is my next ecstasy now?

This might be a good time to talk about poetry and addiction. But instead, let's talk about translation. Let's talk about the joys—and the tonic—of a borrowed intensity, an ecstasy at only one remove. Let's look around, as my darling Apollinaire so often did, for someone or some *ones* loving well. On the invitation of friends, I went one evening, very soon after September 11, 2001, to Treasure Island Hotel and Casino, there to see Cirque du Soleil's "Mystère." I was very skeptical at first, having only sad and seedy recollection of those circuses I'd seen as a boy: derelict tigers; jaundiced and unhappy clowns on rickety stilts. But my friends' enthusiasm was relentless, and so I went. Once the show began, once the flamboyant and extravagant performers took to the air, I began to smile, and I smiled for nearly two whole hours. In the autumn of 2001 I was, like most folks, tired all the time. And at Treasure Island I was reminded: a tired man loves a circus. A tired ecstasy is grateful to shut its inward eye and wake to a spectacle. The dazzle of other human bodies wheeling and capering refreshes a body at rest, and after a while, a passive pleasure in excess might turn to action and to access once again. As Charles Ives wrote in his song "The Circus Band," "Ain't it a grand and glorious noise!" (Joyful and spontaneous too, the way God likes it. Our ecstasies are God's circus after all.)

While I watched Cirque du Soleil, I lived moments breathtaking not from danger but from glee. I felt the tug of transformation not as a change or risk, but as a smile. (Please, my friends, let us never talk about "risk"

in poetry again.) Seeing perfections not my own sustained above empty air, I borrowed conviction from
their flamboyance. Deathlessness at second hand felt
deathless all the same. Ives's song for the circus ends

> Where is the lady all in pink?
> Last year she waved to me I think.
> Can she have died? Can! that! rot!
> She is passing but she sees me not.

Ives's exclamations shout defiance to death and to dejection. When I translate them, circus shouts might
very well transform my words. That's what I'm talking
about. For me, translation is a something borrowed
from a circus.

Or from a garden. The transformative ecstasy of perfect attention, that sublime instance of being alone
with the Alone, suffers exhaustions and dejections of
its own sometimes in aftermath. A tired man also loves
a garden and all the friendship of its ready-made va-
riety. He need not rise, but simply remain level with the
beauties and distractions all around. And who knows?
Distraction might refresh attention, given time. In the
spell of translation, innocence takes a vacation from
the task of innocence, visiting inconsequence, another

garden state. I want to say a little in favor of a translator's Edenic, unabashed selfishness: i.e., that, waking in a garden, it is sometimes entirely all right to exclaim, "What's in it for me?"

A translator is good for himself, and I love translating because, as far as I have found, it is a pastime wholly made of advantages, free of any dangers. A night at the circus. A day in the garden. No matter how poorly *I* perform, no matter how distracted my efforts are by self-interest and prejudice, the originals remain unscathed. I remind you of Ives's exclamation: "Can! that! rot!" Adam did no harm to the Garden, only to himself. (As we have seen, though, and gratefully, attention makes repairs.) The Edenic translator is a compulsory innocent, incapable of significant harms, and innocence is the greatest advantage any man or woman can enjoy. Innocence receives the free gift of amazement. I have translated two volumes of Apollinaire, and he always still amazes me. And so *my* language and *my* sense of a poem's possibilities find themselves *effortlessly* enlarged when I translate him. The sort of innocence enjoyed by translation is never alone. It has ever and ever the company of what it never harms. Translating, I freely enjoy the company of Guillaume Apollinaire and all his sweet instruction. (I am enough of a Calvinist, as I suspect you know, to believe that recreation and instruction, like weariness and fret, are one and the same.) What better tonic could there be for the chronic loneliness of a poet than such Friendship?

(In my innocence, of course I impose my poetic upon my friend and his poems. I have no choice, nor would I wish for one. My poetic is neither method nor craft; it is my way of being in the world. And so I must say here—call it a disclaimer—that it's best for the great poets to have many, many translators. After all, you can never have too many friends.)

(And never—call this a caveat—let the issue of mastery of a foreign language discourage or dissuade you from a spell of translation. You and I shall never master English, for heaven's sake, and so what hope have we of mastering a *second* language. Incompetence is no bar; ask the newborn. Mastery has almost nothing to do with poetry *or* with translation. Style is mishap, a hopefully alluring disproportion. I hope to befriend Apollinaire's asymmetries with my own. And on my own. A green thought in a green shade wants no master, imagines no standard. Translation is play, and play must never be bewitched by mastery. Ask the lonely child. Myself, I play a crazy game of paper chase with my Apollinaire. His poems elude me at the level of the syllable. He taunts me, tenderly, with nuance.

Almost any poet or reader of poetry could summarize his "Zone," could pen its gist into paragraphs or strophes. But to have the pleasure (and liberty) of moving as "Zone" moves, to act out in English its darling misbehaviors, demands a carefree physical attention. No matters of mastery intrude. Or distract. Translation is a behavior, not a knack. John Ashbery (himself a delightful translator—have a look at his versions of Pierre Reverdy and Pierre Martory) has written, "We see us as we truly behave." In translation, this behavior, as is appropriate to a garden state, goes ungoverned and carelessly. Ask a happy child. He enjoys the advantage.)

As young as I was (twenty-seven) in the summer of 1981, I was well and truly exhausted and dejected. I'd completed a PhD at Buffalo and had just finished my first year of full-time teaching at the University of Tennessee. I could look forward to several months of freedom in a green and friendly place, but I could not for the life of me find my way to a poem. I'd had some lovely, early successes, publishing in *Poetry* and in several issues of that wonderful, now alas folded magazine, *Antaeus.* And then? Ridiculous, waste sad time, at least as far as writing was concerned. Everything I did was a paler and poorer duplication of what I'd tried before. Not surprisingly, *Poetry* and *Antaeus* lost interest in me. My eyes were open, but I could hardly see, so frantically was I trying to envision my writing as it had been before. I needed a friend. I needed the loan of a Vision entirely *not* my own. I took to wandering the stacks in the university library, hoping that something would leap out at me. One morning, I saw, at the far end of an aisle in Romance Languages, a bright window looking out onto an especially flamboyant full view of magnolia, that most shameless of trees. I walked toward it, and as I walked my eye fell upon a blue book on the shelf, *Alcools* by Guillaume Apollinaire. I grabbed it up, remembering how much I'd liked Apollinaire in college, and took it with me to the metal desk in the window. I sat down and began to flip through the pages. Coming upon an old favorite, *"Le Pont Mirabeau,"* I read and remembered the pleasures of reading it before. When I looked up, the magnolia was just a little bit greener, a little brighter. As Thoreau one time remarked, on hearing a bird sing at the window of a house of mourning, "Well, one of us is well at any rate." Apollinaire was very well indeed, and I found myself believing poetry was in fact entirely possible, freely available, albeit lately not to me. I'd found a friend. Perhaps I'd have my loan. I took a piece of paper out of my pocket and started to translate— not very seriously, and certainly not very well, but recreationally. I had a good time. And so I decided to come back the next morning to that same metal desk in the library window and do it all over again. For the better part of that summer I kept on translating *"Le Pont Mirabeau"* and intoning, softly, my various versions to Pal Magnolia.

I am not writing about the art of translation, its decisions and compromises, its endless negotiations between sound and sense. I am writing about refreshment and renovation. My summer on the Mirabeau Bridge refreshed my eyes, and what I began to see remade my excitement, my sense of the scope and possibilities of words and lines. I began by finishing a translation that really pleased me.

Mirabeau Bridge

Under Mirabeau Bridge the river slips away
   And lovers
  Must I be reminded
Joy came always after pain

    The night is a clock chiming
    The days go by not I

We're face to face and hand in hand
   While under the bridges

Of embrace expire
Eternal tired tidal eyes

The night is a clock chiming
The days go by not I

Love elapses like the river
Love goes by
Poor life is indolent
And expectation always violent

The night is a clock chiming
The days go by not I

The days and equally the weeks elapse
The past remains the past
Love remains lost
Under Mirabeau Bridge the river slips away

The night is a clock chiming
The days go by not I

What happened? I had found a pair of tired eyes, Apollinaire's, and seen them refreshed by undulations of sound and symmetries of line—i.e., by poetry. On Mirabeau Bridge Apollinaire reminded me that there is no difference between "eye" and "I." An opened eye finds the poem that carries a poet away. A world of eyes transpires in an I. And I stood with Apollinaire for quite a few days that summer, in another('s) world, seeing the time outspeed at light speed, and with the leisure of a river too, a sorrowing I that was he and was I. When, in translating, I came to that phrase "Eternal tired tidal eyes," the library window opened wide, and in the greenness beyond it I began to see a poetry made of eyes. A little less tired and a little less dejected than I'd been in months, I did a poem of my own in thanks to my friend.

Homage

I have looked into the air between my hands
and seen the white ovals, the abstracted, green
or blue eyes of maps of cities. Every face

accuses: the wrong of exile; the worse wrong
of pity, which is like the rain on metal
railings or like the sounds at night that fix

themselves to the shadows of small leaves and change
as the wind changes. I even name them sometimes.
Ellen. Madrid. The one whose eyes were too

close to one another, who was called Berthe.
The naming puts them at a distance and down
to where a thing can be fought for, lost, and then

forgotten easily. In the abandoned,
white cities of a republic, the names are eyes
on walls. The rain, if it rains, makes them luminous.

I have looked into the faces between my hands
And seen years fail. The abandoned cities reclaim
themselves for themselves and shine with exile,
        with pity.

Not bad at all. A little down-at-the-mouth perhaps,
but for me, a wholly new sound and a different kind of
image-making than I'd ever done. I was crazy for eyes,
and seeing them everywhere, just as Apollinaire had
seen them flowing under Mirabeau Bridge, I saw anew.
A recreational exile can be a little ecstasy too. A circus.
A garden. A make believe that makes belief. Translating
is good for you.

Many, many times since that first good summer in
Tennessee I have found myself wanting Apollinaire's
visionary, bright company. I have a real dislike for the
term "writer's block," a term that seems to imply an altogether fictional urgency. Nobody ever needs to write

a poem, and how in the world can an absence prove a present impediment? Whether I write or not, the world continues the effortless composition of itself, as anyone, including myself, can see. No, there's no need of another poem from me, but writing is, despite all my self-righteous disclaimers, a pleasure I prefer to enjoy rather than to remember. And when my writing is altogether familiar, altogether too easy (the words "easy" and "effortless" are, I insist, *not* synonyms) and too entirely intact from the very beginning, I get no pleasure at all. I might as well be emptying the dishwasher, as I do first thing every morning half-asleep. A poet writes when he's awake, and writer's block is merely a sleep-writing, an absence by day and an imposture in its dream. So every so often, for many years now, I've relied upon Apollinaire as upon a wake-up call. When the poem under my hand is a too-familiar dream of itself, a memory in advance and instead of a Vision, I lay that poem aside and take up almost any poem at all by my Guillaume. I translate it then, for the fun of it. And with the fun there always suddenly returns a brightness and the new cadences of brightness that are the sound of light at play within the eye.

> I sang like a man
> I sang my heart out joyfully
> As love awoke in a different year entirely

> (from "The Song of the Poorly Loved")

Daughters of daughters the colors of your eyelids
Flutter and are flowers in a crazy wind

(from "Saffrons")

The old words are dying
Only habit or cowardice
Puts them into poems
. . . .
The word is sudden it is a God quaking
Come closer and sustain me I so deeply
Regret the outstretched hands of those who adored me
What oasis of arms will greet me tomorrow
Do you understand the joy of seeing new things

(from "Victory")

Etc. In the play of translation, time moves forward with
no regard for me, and I am given what I wanted—i.e., a
different day entirely, nothing whatever to do with the
dishwasher. In the play of translation, the color of my
eyes is poured outward and exposed to blessed winds
of blessed change. New words, unadoring but unprecedented, void the old and fill that void with Things, with
phenomena stronger than the imposture of any dream
I'd had that I'd been writing poetry.

And so, via such stints of translation, the pleasures of writing have time and again returned to me. With ears for a new sound, with eyes rinsed clear of shady habit, I could hear a line I'd never written and see a beauty further than I'd known. I suppose that's all that a new poem is, to a poet: a cadence that was always on the wind but only just now heard as a music; an object always to hand but only just now lifted into the sunshine where it shows the eye a shape and shapeliness it had not seen to use. Another poet's words in another language sound a most corrective and refreshing axiom: *it could be otherwise.* Without the altogether unexpected alternative, there is no poetry. And what is translation if not a liberating romp among alternatives? All are intriguing, none is exact. (Sometimes I like to ask my students to translate one of their poems into a nonexistent language of their own invention. With all possibility of accuracy abolished, they find themselves at play among unexacting sounds. Which is to say they find new poems and a broad way out of the old.) All have the allure of an irrevocable decision that matters not at all. (Sometimes I ask my students to take a little piece of music—the *Gymnopedies* of Erik Satie work very well—and translate each and every note into a word. And by this I do not mean for them to compose a lyric for the tune, but, rather, to convert the notes to language. You see, my Calvinism is relentless, even at play. If all goes well and, again, with all possibility of accuracy abolished, the student finds a measure he had never planned and a syntax never diagrammed before. Of course, the music remains entirely untouched, its allure uncompromised.) And I suppose that's what a new poem is to a poet: an allure uncompromised by words.

Some years ago, in a letter to that wonderful poet, translator, and good friend Stephen Berg, I rambled on a bit about my notions of translation and about all the help that my sojourns with friend Apollinaire had given me. In reply, Stephen offered me a challenge and a change. Why not publish some of these translations of mine, and why not include among them a version of Apollinaire's daunting, delightful masterpiece, "Zone"? The change of course was in the very proposal: taking the watershed poem of international Modernism, a poem translated many times by many fine writers, Samuel Beckett most eminent among them, and making my (guilty?) pleasures in its company a matter of more-or-less public record—a text, an aftermath. My make believe would make a vow: this is "Zone;" I am the man; I have seen it; I was there. And the challenge, of course, lay in the preservation of those pleasures despite the unecstatic (or post-ecstatic) pressures of avowal. Would refreshment and sunshine survive the consequences? What would Pal Magnolia say? He'd tell me to have a good time. He'd say to keep it Light. The word "definitive" needn't be defined, nor even mentioned.

And so for almost seven months—happy ones, even though the Guggenheim money that was supposed to have lasted me till summer was altogether spent by Groundhog Day—in an almost empty house at the end of a road on a sunny cove of Lake of the Ozarks *(eaux arc),* I romped through "Zone," making notes, keeping a record. I'm happy to say my pleasures all survived. At every turn, my friend Apollinaire took care of that. As if he'd known I'd be coming, he spoke in his very first line to my circus-hopes and garden of necessities.

A la fin tu es las de ce monde ancien

Just look at that. We begin at the end—*à la fin*—so continuity's not a problem. ("Zone" is the very first poem in Apollinaire's *Alcools* although he wrote it last of all.) There's nothing to carry on, no instructions to follow, no letter of the law. (One of my favorite passages in all the world is by Denise Levertov: "You have come to the shore. There are no instructions." Translation is a day at the beach and, sometimes, many such days.) And we are already intimates, Guillaume and I; he addresses me as *"tu,"* as "thou." He knows that I'm tired—*las*—and that I and my eyes could use some refreshment. I've never been shy about motives. I've come for some recreational exile and a little ecstasy too. My old world—*ce monde ancien*—or any old world, has simply got to go. "Zone" obliges because

At last you're tired of this elderly world

And then the poem, unpunctuated, goes forth: from weariness toward a tender and a playful apocalypse, eyes widening as it goes.

Along the way, refreshment of the eye and renovation of the gaze shape the poem and speed it, even as it strays into unprecedented geographies and loves. No punctuation could complement "Zone's" apocalypse because, for Apollinaire, apocalypse transpires in the eye as it finds new worlds arising and renovated hearts opening into light. Read the poem. I'd love to read it line by line with you now, but this little book has a different row to hoe. I will simply show a few passages in evidence of how, while I translate him, Apollinaire delights my eye and makes my apparent task a playtime. Let's take them, as the telephone operators like to say, in the order in which they are received—

> I saw a pretty street this morning I forgot the name
> New and cleanly it was the sun's clarion

The absolute erasure that is revelation never sounded so gentle or so sure. To see is to forget; I never tire of such news. A vision is a morning, as in "I saw a pretty street this morning." And morning means forgetting, as in "this morning I forgot the name." Early sunshine moves in many directions all at once. Daybreak is uncontrollable. Here's apocalypse in the simplest terms imaginable, terms a child could use, and using them, I become a child. Real eyesight is unprecedented and so escapes all names. As it turns out, the optic nerve is an antinomian. Seeing a pretty street in the morning means that everything is new again. (I grew up in New York, and I remember the very first time I ever walked down Fifth Avenue at six o'clock in the morning. It was unrecognizable, washed so clean with water and silence and sunshine that it might have been Eden before anyone was there.) Light wipes the world clean of worldliness as worldliness is merely shadows in a lazy or a tired eye. Because Apollinaire sees it, it is pretty, and because it is pretty, the street is a New street. And the sun is its clarion, a tocsin, a Gabriel's trumpet blaring the news itself has made. Translating such a passage, I am simplified to where I scarcely need any of my words at all. My friend, since you're a poet yourself, you know how good *that* feels.

And while we are on the subject of angels, it is good to go a little further on in "Zone," there to be met by this line:

Pupille Christ de l'oeil

And in my English:

Christ pupil of the eye

I know that my redeemer liveth. He is the opening in my iris through which the blessed sunshine enters me. Such a simple line (imagine how much George Herbert would have loved it!) hardly taxes the translator's imagination. And that, of course, is the point and the poignancy of finding, then translating such a line. It's so easy, just as my pupil opens easily, without the least effort or any intention of mine. Redemption, refreshment, these are freely available, and no exertion and, indeed, no merit are required. This line (I could so easily say that this entire little book is nothing but a gloss of it) and all its implications explain to me exactly what keeps happening when I translate Apollinaire. My burdens, which are the elderly world of me and the pointless effort of my eyes to see another poem there, disappear. They are carried away by Apollinaire's pious insouciance. It's a pleasure to note that, moving on from "Christ pupil of the eye," the poem describes its ultra-modern Christ as a fabulous airborne aviator, and then it declares:

Les anges voltigent autour du joli voltigeur

In my English:

Angels flutter around the pretty trapeze act

There's that apocalyptic little word "pretty" again, transforming everything, just as it did along an antinomian street (you know, that's not a bad way to think about a line of poetry) quite early in the morning. And didn't I already tell you that translation is a something borrowed from a circus? As it turns out, that something is salvation. Charles Ives could have made a crazy, tender hymn for Apollinaire's Jesus and trapeze. "Can! that! rot!" Well, of course not, not with all those angels hovering round.

Yet "Zone" is a poem of Earth as well as Air, as Apollinaire, that tireless boulevardier, is led by his eye across Paris and then over all of Europe and beyond.

His is an eye-errant, an optic Quixote, whose every glance, backward and forward, catastrophizes everything with angelic tenderness. (Don't forget: Christ is the pupil of his eye, and of yours, and of mine.) A backward glance, through the varnish, darkly:

> Your life is a painting in a dark museum
> And sometimes you examine it closely

Museums are the detritus of light, just as a life, that burdensome sense of one's being as a destiny comprehended and apart, hung on a wall and framed if you like (and oh how busy some poets are with framing), is the detritus of birth and of rebirth. Don't forget: Christ is the pupil of the eye. Whenever we see, we are born again. And when Apollinaire sees his life sequestered in the dark this way, and examines it with his itinerant eye, the upshot is not insight but liberation. Another of the pleasures of translation is simply this: I can walk away from it. Indeed, eventually I must, if I'm going to write any more poems of my own, just as I must walk away from my life if I hope to be reborn. (Don't worry; it's quite all right and even appropriate, here, to think of Rilke's "Archaic Torso of Apollo." But I much prefer Apollinaire; he's got legs.) Immediately, "Zone" exits the museum, as the very next passage shows, in a forward glance, catastrophically:

> You are walking in Paris the women are bloodsoaked
> It was and I have no wish to remember it was the end
>   of beauty

Here's an apocalypse worthy of George Fox, founder of the Society of Friends, whose memoirs record a vision of the shires and townships of Merrie England awash in blood. Outside the museum, in a bath of blood, beauty ends and with it any wish to remember "the end" (ends are purposes too) of beauty. From here forward, beauty will be unprecedented and, perhaps, purposeless too. Freed, however drastically, from every priority, the eye is free to find beauty anywhere it lights. Or nowhere, which is a blessed break from beauty, a chance to abandon the ideal and drift. (Almost a thousand years ago now, another Guillaume, Guillaume of Aquitaine, averred "I shall make a poem of nothing. It came to me while I was sleeping on my horse.") This is a translator's relief and freedom. I can never know Apollinaire's purposes in writing "Zone," and so they do not burden me as my own, all too often, do. Ignorance is a good guide. I can count on it to surprise me. I would never have thought that x or y could be so beautiful, perhaps even the most beautiful lines of poetry I never thought to write—because I didn't. Apollinaire did. And he's not talking. He's walking, just as George Fox did, from one End of the World to another.

The catastrophizing of beauty is a release. Apocalypse makes peace. Now that beauty is no longer an issue, it may be actual, effortless, and very near. As John Ashbery wrote in "And *Ut Pictura Poesis* Is Her Name," (how's *that* for playing fast and loose with ideality!) "Bothered about beauty you have to/Come out into the open . . . /And rest." And rest my Apollinaire surely does. Translation is a something borrowed from a garden, and it is to a garden that "Zone" goes on.

> You are in the garden at an inn outside of Prague
> You are completely happy a rose is on the table
> And instead of getting on with your short-story
> You watch the rosebug sleeping in the rose's heart

What careless pleasure there is to be had with all those prepositions: in, at, outside, on, etc.! What a peaceful gambol and recess, and all while sitting still at a table in a garden. The end of beauty is the beginning of complete happiness. I cannot begin to tell you how surprised and delighted I felt to see those words *"tout heureux"* and to enjoy the effortless task of their translation. I mean, when was the last time you read a poem that declared the poet's complete happiness? And here the happiness is simply a consequence of things as they are: "a rose is on the table." Translation is a consequence of poems already made; "Zone" is a rose I saw on my writing table. As it turns out, the instance of complete happiness is the end of writing too. Apollinaire lays his story aside ("It is even in/prose, I am a real poet"— Frank O'Hara, "Why I Am Not a Painter"), abandoning his intentions and their authorities to his eye. As ever, the eye rewards abandoned efforts, as here, with a "rosebug sleeping in the rose's heart." Rest is given a vision of rest, and the vision is real, entirely simple, near. No need for any writing. The eye provides. Have you read *The Romance of the Rose,* medieval cornerstone of all French poetry? Then you'll recall how many thousands of lines (and how many poets—Jean de Meun had to take up the *Romance* where Guillaume de Lorris broke off) it took the poem to penetrate at last the allegorical rose's heart. Here, Apollinaire's quest succeeds without even beginning. And success looks into a very real sleep.

Refreshed by a vision of refreshment, "Zone" gathers speed and gladness, becoming giddy, almost global in its loves. To read it is to see a cinema of compassions, a kinesis of tender trysts in Marseilles, Koblenz, Amsterdam, Rome, and in the refugee slums and working-men's dives of Paris. Read it, in any translation you can, right now. (It is Christmas as I'm writing.

"Noel sur la terre! as Rimbaud declared.) It will do you good. The eye, unobscured by beauty, unhampered by the identity it left behind in the dark museum, sees— and I cannot see my way clear to say it any way but this—as God sees, i.e., unjudging, heart-broken-apart, and very fast.

Her hands I'd never noticed are hard and cracked

My pity aches along the seams of her belly

I humble my mouth to her grotesque laughter

An opened eye opens the heart. On such occasions, translation is heartbreaking in the most wonderful sense. My English hurries to the scene of Apollinaire's visual abasement, and there it breaks, line break by line break, stanza break by stanza break, opening to admit the poet's unjudging love. You'll remember Jack Spicer: "Poet be like God." Well, when the poetry is as godly as this, such likeness, for this translator, proves even easier than effortless. There's no argument to shape, no rhetoric to transpose into a different decorum. There is only vision and the immediate response to vision, entirely visual itself. Godliness sacrifices everything for this. And so does poetry. Translation goes along for the ride.

Sacrifice is the natural circumstance of light. It gives
itself away. It is gives *everything* away to the eye that
sees it and gives everything it shows. It never slows
or withholds. It could scarcely do so and still be light.
When the poet is Apollinaire, the sacrifices of translation (in Heaven, Henny Youngman says, "Take my
eyes, please!"), the surrender of one's gifts to another,
the suspension of one's own purposes in poetry, are as
nothing. That's what I mean by "effortless." Translating
"Zone," I didn't do anything at all, but something
happened for which I am ever grateful. (And grateful to Stephen too, for the challenge and the change.)
"Zone" ends:

Sun cut throated

"Zone" ends in the circumstance of light itself: a sun—
its throat slit as though it were an animal upon the
altar of the ancients, a lambkin in an elderly world—
sacrificed to be seen. Finding myself awash in the sunshine with Pal Magnolia and Pal Apollinaire, I do not
translate. I am translated.

Scholium #4—Translating Is Good for You

Here's a passage from "Rosalind and Helen: A Modern Eclogue," one of the very last poems that Percy Bysshe Shelley began in England, prior to his life in Italy.

> In silence then they took the way
> Beneath the forest's solitude.
> It was a vast and antique wood,
> Thro' which they took their way;
> And the gray shades of evening
> O'er that green wilderness did fling
> Still deeper solitude.

Conventions are proposed as perceptions—"gray shades of evening;" "green wilderness." Exaggeration suborns emphasis. What "wood" is "vast?" Anthropomorphism mutes the wild. Shelley is one of the greatest sound technicians in the canon, and we can hear these lines working to weave a music with perfect and imperfect rhymes more intricate than English tetrameters conventionally allow. But it's work. The lines labor, and the eye has nothing to see but their idea: "a still deeper solitude."

Shelley was wildly prolific in Italy, doing virtually all of his best writing there, including along the way translations of Homer and Virgil, Plato, Cavalcanti, Goethe and Dante. The change of scenery and, I reckon, the change of languages too, was good for him. Here's part of a passage he did from *Purgatorio.* (I love the fact that Shelley most often translated bits and pieces of this or that; he was having fun.) It's from Canto XXVIII, the scene of Matilda Gathering Flowers.

My slow steps had already borne me o'er
Such space within the antique wood, that I
Perceived not where I entered any more,—

When, lo! a stream whose little waves went by,
Bending towards the left through grass that grew
Upon its bank, impeded suddenly

My going on. Water of purest hue
On earth, would appear turbid and impure
Compared with this, whose unconcealing dew,

Dark, dark, yet clear, moved under the obscure
Eternal shades, whose interwoven looms
The rays of moon or sunlight ne'er endure.

I moved not with my feet, but mid the glooms
Pierced with my charmèd eye . . .

Yes, indeed, there's that "antique wood" again, but here it is truly be-wildernessed. And the music weaves a watercourse through wild enjambments, leading the eye, the charmed eye. Idea is the pure evidence of effortless perception: "unconcealing dew." A matter-of-fact intricacy makes this passage shine.

When he died, Shelley was engaged upon a long poem, "The Triumph of Life," whose shape and sound are glad beneficiaries of the poet's pleasures with Dante. These are some lines from the opening:

>   . . . the deep
>
> Was at my feet, and Heaven above my head,—
> When a strange trance over my fancy grew
> Which was not slumber, for the shade it spread
>
> Was so transparent, that the scene came through
> As clear as when a veil of light is drawn
> O'er evening hills they glimmer; and I knew
>
> That I had felt the freshness of that dawn
> Bathe in the same cold dew my brow and hair,
> And sate as thus upon that slope of lawn

Under the self-same bough, and heard as there
The birds, the fountains and the ocean hold
Sweet talk in music through the enamoured air . . .

Transparency is a revelation here and, as Dante showed, a vision of the sovereign Real. These lines glimmer with particular, near, and tender perception: "freshness;" "*cold* dew;" "*slope* of lawn." Here is a complex occasion known as Creation, whose complexity is a pleasure, not a puzzlement, and whose instance is prelude to Shelley's last, best ecstasy. No need to finish what never means to end.

In Modern poetry, nobody can hold a candle (or a halo) to Ezra Pound when it comes to the recreational wildness of translation. The Idaho Kid was always recreating himself, and the catalyst of his countless transformations was always the new sound of a new light changing his eye. He began as a Pre-Raphaelite has-been, by his own confession "Wrong from the start."

What hast thou, O my soul, with paradise?
Will we not rather, when our freedom's won,
Get us to some clear place wherein the sun
Lets drift in on us through the olive leaves
A liquid glory?

(from "Blandula, Tenulla, Vagula")

Here, sunlight has almost no light-speed at all. It oozes. And clarity sits still. This is the sort of artificial Paradise dismantled by Wallace Stevens in "Sunday Morning," and I can almost see the dust gathering on those un-alive olive leaves. Light, when it is real, is entirely motion, and real trees live and die in it, and on it too. Thank heaven, Ezra learned as much and more from his visits with Li Po.

> The leaves fall early this autumn, in wind.
> The paired butterflies are already yellow with August
> Over the grass in the West garden,
> They hurt me.
> I grow older . . .

> *(from "The River-Merchant's Wife: A Letter")*

> And once again, later, we met at the South bridge-
>   head.
> And then the crowd broke up, you went north to
>   San palace,
> And if you ask how I regret that parting:
>   It is like the flowers falling at Spring's end
>   Confused, whirled in a tangle.

> *(from "Exile's Letter")*

All emotion here is evidenced by motion: it falls; it breaks; it whirls. Its medium is light and air, matters for the eye as it remakes a mind in lines of letters. The epistolary Eye, Li Po's greatest gift. And Pound was quick to learn how to quicken his lines, moving fast from *Cathay* to the early *Cantos* where speed of light makes all the sound. This is from "Canto IV:"

> The valley is thick with leaves, with leaves, the trees,
> The sunlight glitters, glitters a-top,
> Like a fish-scale roof,
> > Like the church roof in Poictiers
> If it were gold.
> > Beneath it, beneath it
> Not a ray, not a sliver, not a spare disc of sunlight
> Flaking the black, soft water;
> Bathing the body of nymphs, of nymphs, and Diana,
> Nymphs, white-gathered about her, and the air, air.
> Shaking, air alight with the goddess,
> > fanning their hair in the dark,
> Lifting, lifting and waffing:
> Ivory dipping in silver,
> > Shadow'd, o'ershadow'd
> Ivory dipping in silver,
> Not a splotch, not a lost shatter of sunlight.

Light shatters to show itself. And what does it show? That air is air, and everything's moving there. Paradise is nothing wasted on the eye. Li Po was Ezra Pound's picture palace.

Scholium #5—Translation Is a Behavior Not a Knack

In "Canto XIII," the first of his Confucian cantos, Pound recounts a story of the great sage putting a question to each of his young disciples. When they had answered,

> And Kung smiled upon all of them equally.
> And Thseng-sie desired to know:
>> "Which had answered correctly?"
> And Kung said, "They have all answered correctly,
>> "That is to say, each in his nature."

Nature is the behavior of evidence. Translating, naturally, is one such behavior, a showing-forth of a reading and of a reader, making changes, being changed. Here's a very short, very famous passage from Rimbaud's *Une Saison en Enfer:*

> O saisons, ô châteaux!
> Quelle âme est sans défauts?

> J'ai fait la magique étude
> Du bonheur, qu'aucun n'élude.

Two couplets in rough trimeter, and nothing complicated. But humanness is ever a complexity underway, illuminated by actions. Translation is one such, and every one of the translations I've seen of these four lines has, one way or another, complicated them. And by this I do not mean "obscured" them. No. I mean to say that each has added another pair of eyes and so another portion of the tender chaos that is Vision. This is Wallace Fowlie:

> O seasons, O castles!
> What soul is without flaws?

> I have made the magic study
> Of happiness which no man evades.

Entirely accurate and unmistakably singular. (In translation, 1+1 is another; hence the changes.) Chateaux have become castles, have been thus fortified. Translations sometimes feel the need to defend themselves. In my own poems, I can hide inside my subjectivity. But in translating poems by someone else, my subjectivity is utterly exposed and objectified. There's no faulting Fowlie for trading elusiveness for evasion. A translator does not escape; he steps aside. He is literally beside himself, a 1+1, another pair of eyes. And here's another, Enid Rhodes Peschel's:

> O seasons, O châteaux!
> What soul is quite unflawed?

> I have pursued the magic lore
> Of happiness, which all explore.

Uncastellated, this Rimbaud is a decorous ("*quite* un-flawed") mage, smooth ("unflawed") at the margin, and confident, pursuing, not failing to elude the "lore." Peschel's Rimbaud is the incomparable philomath, the perfect schoolboy who took romance to its un-perfecting extreme. This translation dotes and loves. It is the warmest I have seen, and in many ways the most brave, the least shy to show its loving. If I did not love Apollinaire, for example, what on earth would *I* be doing here?

And then there's Charles Olson. He was large, he con-tained multitudes. And one of them was Rimbaud, here taken into Olson's "Variations Done for Gerald Van De Wiele:"

> . . . (O saisons, o chateaux!
> Délires!
>   What soul
> is without fault?

> Nobody studies
> ḥappiness

Not translating—O saisons, o chateaux!—is the most translating. And to Rimbaud's words Charles Olson adds another favorite of Rimbaud's, albeit from elsewhere: "Délires." 1+1 is elsewhere too. *Une Saison en Enfer* awakes to find itself in another poem entirely whose author is a "nobody" added. Olson's signature behavior is ever to make of negative capability a bear hug, a thumping, dancing embrace. Here, American white space sets the original French to new and different motion, and the motion is only Olson's nature, moving "correctly," as human natures do.

Scholium #6—I Am Translated

In Apollinaire's *"Le Voyageur"* ("The Traveler"), there is a passage whose simplicity is so enigmatic that I think about it almost every single day. I've translated it this way:

> Can you remember anyone in these photographs
> Remember the day a bee fell in the fire

"Le Voyageur" cascades from friendship to friendship; its memories travel with many companions, all of whom are intimates and none of whom is named. There's something so warm and close in this showing of photographs that my never knowing their content scarcely matters at all. I have pictures of my own, and it is those Apollinaire shows in the intimate space, the intimate moment created by never knowing me. And then there is the inexhaustible mystery of "the day a bee fell in the fire." Of course I don't remember it; I wasn't there; I hadn't been born yet. And still Apollinaire expects that I will, and his poem depends on it. Trust is always rewarded, and because the bee is not a metaphor but an occasion, it continues with its day to my days. Apollinaire has given me an eye for bees and an abid-

ing trust in their momentousness. He has also given me a poem of my own called "Picnic."

> The story of my life is untrue but not
> Thanksgiving Day when the bee fell in the bottle.
> All days take instruction from accident.
> My wife opened the red wine in a good spot
> We'd found as we were hiking along a dry
> Creekbed. She filled our cups as I cut
> Bread and apples. We saw the bee dive
> Into the green bottleneck and start
> To swim. Then we spoke about children and ways to move
> An old piano north to where our nephews live.
> We finished the wine, and the bee was still alive.
> I tapped him onto the ground, and he walked off
> Untangling antennae from wings and wine.
> We hurried to reach the car while there was still daylight.

Almost nothing happens in my poem. Claudia and I go on little picnics all the time, and this particular time we were simply escaping the crowded confines of the family trailer in Hemet, California, on a noisy holiday. But Apollinaire had long since given me an eye for bees, and whenever a bee falls, I pay attention. And attention, as I have urged so often, is how a poem begins. I like to think my "Picnic" is a thoughtful piece and worthwhile. If I'm right, it's because of some photographs I never saw and a bee that died before I was born; a bee that, nevertheless, shared our wine one noisy Thanksgiving.

Intermission: February 1, 2005

It is the deep midwinter. My students are in a funk.
Hours of daylight are precious few, and those we get are
darkened by stinging cold inversions that turn the air
to murk and turn the sun itself into a glaucous eye un-
seeing and adrift. The triumphalist second inaugural of
George W. Bush has just wound down, and in its wake
an air of futility hangs in the classrooms. My students
want to know if there is any purpose in writing poems
at all. Are they merely talking to themselves and to a
coterie of the like-minded and marginalized? At times
like these, they are all too prone to fall prey to foolish
notions that, somehow, more people would read, more
people would be moved and changed by poetry if only
we were to write it differently (and for some reason
"differently" almost always involves traditional rhyme
and meter), if only we were more concerned with communication and a little less with ecstasy, if our imperative were the salvation of the world and not our souls.
And at times like these, I could easily send them to
Robert von Hallberg's wonderful book, *American
Poetry and Culture,* there to see the research proving
that the audience for American poetry, as a percentage
of population, has remained virtually constant since
Whitman's day. Surely, none of us, despondency and

President Bush notwithstanding, is prepared to repeal that most beautiful amendment to the United States Constitution, "Song of Myself." So, more to the point and immediately, I send my friends instead to a letter that D. H. Lawrence wrote to a Mrs. Hopkin in June of 1912. Here is how it ends:

> You might write to us here. Our week of honey-
> moon is over. Lord, it was lovely. But this—do I like
> this better?—I like it so much. Don't tell anybody.
> This is only for the good to know. Write to us.

Poetry is the honeymoon of my eyes, and when the honeymoon is over, I am even more at home in the world. *Of course* "this is only for the good to know." We find our ecstasies for the joy of ecstasy. We save our souls for our souls' sake. And why do we write the poems too? For the refreshment of the courage of the good. Spring is coming. There has never been a President of these United States. If you don't believe me, put my book down for today and reread "Song of Myself." It was written to refresh the courage of the good.

III

Eyesight is prophetic instantly. Writing, sometimes, takes a little bit longer, but it's an eyesight all the same, prophetic in a while. I suggested that you take a break and read once more America's sovereign and signature poem, "Song of Myself." Since then, a dozen weeks have passed and *Pennyweight Windows,* my new & selected poems, has appeared. A happy course of little celebrations is underway in my world, beginning a few days ago in Wisconsin where I was grateful to attend the premiere of American composer Elizabeth Billington Fox's *In Arcady: Nine Songs on Poems by Donald Revell.* The music was wonderful, and it was a wholly new heaven to me to hear my old words in such and several voices, Elizabeth's piano purest among them. And then next morning, through a corridor of thunderstorms, I headed home. At the tiny airport in La Crosse, the lone security man took an instant dislike to me and decided to search my baggage with vehement scrutiny. I always travel with three little books: a green Bible, a green abridgment of Thoreau's *Walden,* and Penguin's pocket edition of "Song of Myself" with Whitman's rakish 1855 portrait on the front. This latter the security man held up to my face; and then he asked me (I swear it) "What are *you* doing with a bodybuilding magazine?" I told him that it belonged to my son, and then he let me go. And so it came to pass that my suggestion to you back in February was prophetic, after a while, and brings us now to the occasion of *Pennyweight Windows.* I want to end this little book with a walk-through, a testing and survey of my own poetry according to the various precepts we've been trying and applying heretofore. Shoulder your duds, and I will mine.

In my first book, *From the Abandoned Cities,* there's a poem called "Here to There." (The piece turns out to have been prophetic in its own incredibly slow way too; twenty years later I finished a collection called *My Mojave,* and it was divided into just two sections: "Here" and "There." Location's inescapable.) The poem, like so much of my early work, is captive to clusters of spatial metaphor emphasized with dogged precision by dour iambics. Still, it begins to begin to anticipate the blessed access of eyesight. Here's stanza one:

> The biggest part of any story is rooms
> and the things inside them. Everything else is too
> vague, too uncertain in the way it happens,
> changes or recites the lines it was
> created to recite to live on its own.
> I have a picture of an old friend naked,

her head tilted into shadow like
an Odalisque's. Whenever I look at it,
I remember first the room that it was taken in,
then her. I see the photograph
of a Brancusi head I'd tacked to the wall
behind her, then hers, tilted into shadow.
That lost room and the tacked-up photograph
keep her alive the way a mirror keeps
a ghost. Their strength is the reality
she uses. Seeing them, I see her live.

Like most young men, I was terrified of change, i.e., of life, and so imagined the work of creation to be a kind of clinging to wreckage and all of poetry a tuneful raft of the Medusa. I imagined that objects had the power to still the eye and to keep it safely apart from the flooding light in shadowlands of memory and little constructs. (My ten-year-old son, God bless him, barged into my workroom a minute ago and asked me, "What is a 'dildo'?" I handed him a dictionary, and a minute later I could hear him giggling in the hallway. See what I mean?) The open eye is naked and Edenic, but in "Here to There" nudity, even the nudity of a dear friend, is unreliable, uncomfortable. And so it must be translated, clothed in metaphor—the more aesthetic, the more sequestered from anything that might actually happen next, the better. Hence the Odalisque. And then the room, the stanza, goes free, remembering only itself and the strict arrangement upon which its authority entirely depends. Its every movement is illusory, and so it moves at leisure from illusion into shadow and back again. The poem is the tourist of itself. Its gaze breaks off at every threshold. Its look, proud captive to memory, proceeds to see no one at all but a photograph, a black-and-white reproduction of a metal woman's head that isn't there. It's a young man's paradise: a surround of motionless women, all absent, all vacated. Voyeurism is antithetical to eyesight; it adventures nothing, while vision enjoys exposure without end.

If the room, as my poem says, is "lost," then where's the photograph? And if the room and photograph together keep my naked friend alive, God help my friend. (She's fine.) Reading this poem of mine after an interval of so many years, I am cheered to think of a beautiful phrase from W. H. Auden's magnificent "The Fall of Rome:" "altogether elsewhere." That's it exactly! Where's the room? Elsewhere, which is to say Binghamton, New York. Where's the Brancusi? Elsewhere, which is to say Philadelphia. And where's my friend? She is altogether, which is to say intact, safely beyond the wishful dismemberment of metaphors more than twenty years behind her time, which is now, which is flooding elsewhere. Poetry always celebrates the collapse of empire, the woebegone imperium of poems. My stanza is a ruin haunted by itself. Its objects, thank Heaven, remain at large. As Auden proposed:

> Altogether elsewhere, vast
> Herds of reindeer move across
> Miles and miles of golden moss,
> Silently and very fast.

How does a poet survive, and gladly, the fall of empires, i.e., the end or dissipation of his authority? He looks away to where the wild things are, learning there that all real things are wild. In "Here to There" I wanted very much to see my friend again. Nothing wrong with that, I guess, except there's no such place as "again," no such occasion in this actual world. Saying, as I did, "I see her live," was a fib: well-intentioned in its wish, but a fib. I wanted eyes, but would not open mine. Isolation, even in the seraglios of blank-verse memory, is a poor recourse to loneliness. Emotion recollected in tranquillity sounds like spooks to me. Frank O'Hara would have picked up the phone. To see, I should have gone looking for what a line might find.

I had lots to learn. With eyes wide shut, as Stanley Kubrick showed, I chose interiority with every word. The poem ends this way:

As in the theater, where stage, props, scenery
pre-exist the action of a play
and outlast it and can bring it back, our rooms,
made into places by the events they've sponsored,
represent the mystery of how
things live and make us live. The origins
of change, they stand still, conduct what enters them.
My friend is what her picture lets her be.
What I remember is what the room, or rather
what that corner of it I can see
keeps. Everything between us returns there
when it returns. Our story, or anything
that happens, happens as the interval
between one stillness and another. Rooms
fix an itinerary of still points
at the two ends of memory and join them.

That opening simile propounds a darkness as well as a play: i.e., the lights of a theater dim so as to permit no bright distraction from illusions underway. My poem depends upon an uncontested priority—a circumstance, a nudity known only to me, in my possession, so to speak—and an enigmatic posterity, "The mystery of how/things live." And that is both its trouble and, I am almost embarrassed to say, its strength. After all, "Here to There" is the poem my editor chose to excerpt on the dust jacket, the poem she believed, and rightly so, most representative of the collection as a whole. And what does it represent? A fierce and formal insistence upon representation: a nudity on paper; a mystery on stage (although in this case, as in the case of so many such poems, the stage is blocked out into stanzas fixed and final). Such insistent representation always forwards the art of poetry as Compulsion: "My friend is what her picture *lets* her be" [italics mine, at last]. Compulsion freezes change at the point of origin. It allows a poet the leisure and license of irrelevance. It allows the reader rest. That opening simile guarantees the fictionality of all that follows. It promises eloquence even as it bars the door (mixing metaphors is a good way of getting rid of the damned things) against ecstasy. Could I have written that stanza, I wonder, had I loved then as I love now the following passage from Robert Creeley's "Could write of fucking:"

> . . . I hate the metaphors.
> I want you. I am still alone,
> but want you with me.

Of course not. I could never, back then, have recognized such an *im*pulse, could never have allowed my words to be carried away so nakedly, so impulsively. Part of what I am trying to chart in this final chapter is a movement in my writing (I cannot call it "progress"—

that's for you to say) away from the poetry of compulsion and outward, in the direction of impulse, in the
direction of a poetry better measured in quanta than
in feet. Compulsion thrives on stillness, and light is
never still. Sight itself requires motion in the eye.
Compulsion conducts itself in the closed spaces, and
"Here to There" is a veritable catalog of these: the
closed space of the iamb and all its lulling insistence;
the closed space of the pentameter whose symmetries are proud (and careful) to be mistaken for natural
speech; the closed spaces of stanzas, stolid in number,
solid upon periods; and most dangerous, most aggressive of all, the closed spaces that confine real objects to
symbolic drudgery. I mean, why didn't that photograph
of an old friend naked get up and run for its life (which,
in fact, though not in my fiction, it truly did)? Why did
I not wish to see my friend anywhere but in the theater of "again"? Why? Because I wanted my poem to
be compelling, and compulsion only works in the dark
backward of irrelevance and rest, "an itinerary of still
points/at the two ends of memory." Under compulsion,
priority and posterity collapse upon each other, and the
poem becomes, as I've suggested, a ruin haunted by itself. There's nothing ruined in Robert Creeley's asser-
tion, nothing arithmetic. Solitude, under the impulse
of desire, may just become numerous, and then it isn't

lonesome anymore. Metaphors, symbols, and all such compulsions, block the light and bar the door.

Please remember that I'm not speaking here of a distinction between formal and free verse. (I've never been able to find one, anyway, and then, who's counting?) I am speaking of, I am looking for, an authority uninsistent and incandescent, an authority unlikely to be deserted by its circus animals because it never once imagines itself nor wishes to be confined to little rings inside a tent or ever to hold the bullwhip of a ringmaster in his fancy dress. My poem "Here to There" is a tight little theater and a tidy circus too. The jointure of its final line shows perfect closure but, alas, no marriage. Nothing shows *through* the poem. Symbols and metaphors make for spectral unions, compelling enough where the lights are dim. Daylight is an impulse to vision—e.g., "I am still alone,/but want you with me"—whose great divorcing command (in his essay "The Doctrine and Discipline of Divorce" John Milton wildly opined that God began to create the universe when he *divorced* the darkness from the light), whose wildest impulse, marries more than two.

Closures without marriage and marriage without union seemed to be the trajectory of my writing for quite a few years beyond the appearance of *From the Abandoned Cities.* Poetry more and more became for me an insistence against any lights other than my own and, thus, a blindness. What form could not compel it might, by the greater exercise of form, confine, at least in the imaginary enclaves of symmetry and total syntax. Callow but adept (American poetry in the 1980s was besotted with both characteristics, at least in the mindset of my ambitions), I thought to find my way clear of change by complicating its every issue to the point of intransigence. Mass vs. transformation—one of the more jejune futilities of my twentieth century. I mean, just listen to me: as I write of it even now, my vocabulary goes over the moon. Although I already loved him, I would not mind my Uncle Ezra:

(To break the pentameter, that was the first heave)

(from "Canto LXXXI")

Not for me. What pentameter could not do alone might yet be accomplished by pentameters wound more tightly than ever upon forms more rigorous than the will to change. Only a writer with eyes wide shut and shouting to himself in empty rooms could credit such forms, but that was me. I began my second collection, *The Gaza of Winter,* in Ripon (pronounced "rippin"), Wisconsin, birthplace of the Republican Party and home to Ripon College. I found myself alone in an enormous house, the only rental property in town, with a ballroom forty feet long and two staircases: one chandeliered and winding, and one, built for servants I believe, lightless and steep. The architect had clearly never heard of Heraclitus: "the way up and the way down are one in the same." Neither, in retrospect, apparently had I. And there I sat in my one good chair, the still point at the center of a crumbling edifice, shouting into the typewriter, stanza by stanza, insistent ceremonies of slow and then slower time. (Uncle Ezra, I really could have used a visitation from your "Gods of the winged shoe" then.) Having long admired the compulsive mischief of sestinas, I decided one morning (it might as well have been evening in the snowbound, claustral town) to complicate that mischief and to extend compulsion by one insistent motive more. Why not? I had a ballroom and two stairwells after all. If you cannot fill it, clutter it. If you will not move, then sink more deeply into your only comfy chair. I wrote the title poem of *The Gaza of Winter* working the measures of my "septina" on Miltonic grist.

> The frail smoke and virtues of the season blind
> us, almost with hands, and which of us can instruct
> the other now? I will have to find your body

shifting at the edge of your last word.
You will have to find whatever I could mean
by groping along that same edge. And all of winter
will be ground to nothing in a slow mill

of smoke and virtue. We are bound to that mill,
and our cold seeking and shifting is the blind
set task of that bondage, cruellest in winter.
What does it matter that we love and instruct
our hearts rightly? I have lost the way to your body.
You have lost the way to know what I mean
when I curl up inside every word

you speak as if it were your hand . . .

In millwork, despair and exercise are one and the same.
In millwork, words and flesh become the interchangeable currencies of a belabored mean. And in millwork,
blindness serves as second sight, that spectral inwardness, instructing the worker to go forward even as
he gets nowhere in this world. In the divorce essay,
Milton writes of "grinding at the mill of a servile copulation." In my septina, I go on to avow that " a marriage is Gaza," where the copulative end-words uncouple
themselves at every turn, meaning to continue nothing
they've begun.

Let's see. The seven inwoven and repeating words of my poem serve as foundation and limit, credo and enclosure of everything it goes on to say. In a sense, they *are* the poem, and all the other words simply whisper in between instances of their emphatic mass. And the first is *blind*, meaning, in the crazy decorum of such a form, that it will also be the last. From blindness to blindness, then, the poem chooses to go. Millwork! Such formalism elevates denial to epic in a kind of stately fever dream. Although I did not know it, in the ramshackle of "The Gaza of Winter" I set out to find the antipode of the poetry of attention. And, if it does not sound too altogether vain, I think I found it. The way up and the way down, one and the same— although I know I did not know it. In my septina, reading does not free the eye, but, rather, freezes it. It waits to watch. The seven repeating words are banana peels upon an empty stage; you just can't take your eyes off them; all you do is wait to watch the other words trip, or not trip, on them. In slapstick, either outcome is always hilarious; if the comic falls, you laugh, you monster you; and if, at the very last moment, he steps over the peel with exaggerated alacrity into perfect safety, you laugh your vicarious approbation. In poetry, alas, either outcome is at best ironic. Should the language stumble into nonsense, form mocks form. The poem as joke. And if, at the very last moment, language cannily o'ersteps its physical fact, form triumphs in a void. The poem as vapor. "Frail smoke" prevails indeed.

Instruct. There is no question of instruction. Waiting to watch, no one is really there to answer. Nobody's reading, not yet. And of course, in the poem's fever dream, a next moment never ever comes. Less than rhetorical, the question is futile. Inattention depends upon futility for its vindication. When Aristotle stands on his head, his pants fall up. But not on earth, so not delighting anybody there.

Body. In such mass, inertly out of reach, body does not move, and only bodies in motion can marry. That's what attention is as I recall: the eye married to motion. Poetry is a darling velocity. Not weighted down by words, it swings. They swerve. "Clinamen."

Word. "Clinamen" means spontaneous, unpredictable deviation, the very thing upon which poems depend for their updraft into poetry. The spontaneities of my septina are all rehearsed, right down to the level of the syllable. The comic did not spontaneously trip on the peel. He planned to. Just as you'd been planning to laugh ever since the curtain rose to reveal it. Form, in "The Gaza of Winter," welters in prediction. Deviation, which is to say the matter of motion, its erotic trace, is endlessly delayed. When flesh becomes word, all the boys are relieved—my former self included. In this sense, my poem colludes with the Council of Nicea.

Mean. Under rubrics, meaning antedates attention. Although I've hidden it, I'm asking the reader not to find I've nothing to hide. I'm asking him to close his eyes and look at me. And then I mean to say, at some length, just how tragic invisibilty is. Do you remember James Joyce's hilarious great sentence? "I am the boy that can enjoy invisibility." That was me. The art that conceals art is just plain mean.

Mill. Which brings us back to servile copulation. The grist "will be ground to nothing." Servitude pretends to mastery in my poem. Emptied in advance by a compulsive and then a compulsory anticipation (what else is there to look forward to but the same words over again?), the words become the ciphers of themselves. And for the manipulation of ciphers, what have I to show? A groping without hands . . . a blindness without eyes . . . winter indoors. A hypertrophied servility slides by on grease.

And so, at the antipode of attention, language can be made to darken a darkness and to empty a cipher, a something less than "zero at the bone." But with the perfect equipoise of Heraclitus, it is equally just to say that "the way *down* and the way up are one and the same." For me, in my Wisconsin's enormous rooms, only excess could moderate my formal compulsion. Only the exaggeration (though, perhaps, "exacerbation" would be the more accurate word) of compulsive closure, via such callow one-upsmanship as a "septina," could break the spell my inattention had me under. What I could not find good sense or courage to discard I could, unknowingly, destroy—at least in my own eyes. The poem ends this way:

> . . . In our first winter,
> I followed you up the steps to where your body
> slipped out of gray ice and lit the mean
>
> rooms wonderfully. What would happen if those mean
> rooms turned up again, a few steps from the mill
> we turn? Would anything about them instruct
> us in how to live there as we did, all winter,
> curled up in the smoke and virtue of blind
> first nights and first days? I wish that every word
> I knew were a step back to them. A body
>
> should give off more than light if anybody
> is to go on thinking of it not meaning

to go crazy. I should do more with the words
I know than make puzzles. A life's work can instruct
a life or can lead it in bondage to a mill
of bad marriage, bad silence, and a blind
refusal to accept that in one winter

everything can go right, then wrong. The winter
I followed you up your steps is over. Your body
is wrapped in its own words now and cannot mean
what I wish it did. I think of years of mill
work ahead, grinding down a store of words
you will not hear me say, living to instruct
a puzzled heart in how to live blind.

Which is to say "What have I done?" Or, to borrow a
more pointed rebuke from John Ashbery, "Just look at
the mess you've made." The circumlocutions of desire
deprive desire doubly. My method deprives me here of
the body I would love and then a second, further time,
of a body to love *with*, i.e., my own. Bodies must live
and move. Words must live and move if they mean to
happen, i.e., to enter the hap of actual, unpredicted
time where all the bodies are. By the time I found myself writing, "I should do more with the words/I know
than make puzzles," I was paying at least a preliminary
kind of attention. I was beginning to know what I was
not doing. Reluctantly but really, my poem confesses

the sovereignty of time. Winters end. Otherness is otherness and not to be compromised or captivated by
eloquence, that insane constellation of banana peels.
The formalism of a poem like "The Gaza of Winter"
is nothing more than wishful thinking, and nothing is
more inattentive and, ultimately, more ungrateful than
a wish. Everything has a future, has "years . . . ahead."
Only the wishing can make their sovereign, spontaneous deviations into millwork. In "The Gaza of Winter"
I followed the instruction of Sir Philip Sidney's Muse—
"look in thy heart and write"—to its literal extreme. It
was dark in my heart, my compulsive Wisconsin. I had
no eyes there, and I needed too many words to say so.
Eventually, I did.

So many times I have been told by loving friends and
family: "You need a new outlook." They've always been
right. If I was to write any poems beyond the hallucinatory inscapes of *The Gaza of Winter,* I'd need to get
out a little more. I'd need to find in form a ruin *not* to
be haunted, a point of departure. And insofar as every
departure presumes an origin, I needed to go home. I'd
leave from there.

In *New Dark Ages,* I found myself awash in leave-
taking, preparing as I and as everybody, whether they
thought of it or not, was, to say good-bye to the twenti-

eth century—that beloved miscreant made of years, the
only years we'd known. (But this is not the place, being
an *ars poetica,* for such thematics, although, in writing this little book, I've come to see that my enterprise
is indistinguishable from autobiography. As Laurence
Olivier says at the end of one of my favorite movies,
The Ebony Tower, "the painter and the paintings, old
cock: can't be split.") What lay ahead was an unimagi-
nable number 2 (counting beyond 1 is the adventure of
vision), a light at the end of what I was only beginning
to think of as a tunnel. (One of the things I've been rail-
ing against in all these pages is tunnel vision, that "eyes
on the prize" mentality that leaves so many poems un-
found and so many gods unworshipped along the way.)
So now, after the passage of some more years, after the
advent of **2**, I am happy to note that my favorite among
all the poems in my third collection is "The Northeast
Corridor," a title taken from newspeak and describing
that cindery ganglion of railways between Boston to
the north and D.C. to the southern end. Ripon, for me,
had come to a very bad end, and I was pining for the
accents and attitudes of home, i.e., New York City and
environs. The poem begins and, in its chatty haphazard
way, begins again and again, under reconstruction in
the remodeling of Pennsylvania Station. I'm in the station bar, "The Iron Horse" of course, drinking whiskeys
poured out by a bartender so much like the northeast

corridor's poet laureate, John Cheever, that he had to
have *been* John Cheever, and waiting for a train to my
sister's house in the Jersey suburbs.

> The bar in the commuter station steams
> like a ruin, its fourth wall open
> to the crowd and the fluttering timetables.
> In the farthest corner, a television
> crackles a torch song and a beaded gown.
> She is my favorite singer, dead when I was born.
> And I have been waiting for hours for a train,
> exhausted between connections to small cities,
> awake only in my eyes finding shelter
> in the fluttering ribbon of shadow
> around the dead woman singing on the screen.
> Exhaustion is a last line of defense
> where time either stops dead or kills you.
> It teaches you to see what your eyes see
> without questions, without the politics
> of living in one city, dying in another.

Here's the passage where Vision intervenes on me,
where a way of making poems gives way to one of finding them just there, in the very last ditch of waiting. In
my case, exhaustion proved to be the inspiration of a
lifetime. (Even though I cannot find it in myself to like
Philip Larkin, I love him for saying "Deprivation is to

me what daffodils were to Wordsworth.") I'm in the bar, the ur-locale of sedentary stirring, waiting to commute, i.e., to be transported by strangers according to a schedule not my own. My poem begins in helplessness already perfected and in a haplessness with plenty of time to spend. (Protracted over time, helplessness equals always either despair or poetry; imperfect helplessness is a bug on the garage floor; perfected through no fault of its own, it is a butterfly.) Thanks to no demolition of mine, the bar's wide open to supernumerous flexions of space and time, the rapid and not-so-rapid transit of late hours and hurried folks. The dead sing while the living go; past and future bend their various intents across connections. Going nowhere for a while, I can see them all as the eyesight goes out of me, seeking shelter from itself in them.

I could easily fall upon a pun here, and so I will. It may be the oldest pun of all, at least among poets: i.e., between "I" and "eye." To my mind, vision is the recourse of eyesight from identity, from habitual inattention (inattention enthralls the eye), from the illegitimate sovereignty of self. This, in my own life and writing, is a conclusion I could not leap to. Traherne did. Blake did. Ronald Johnson did. Me, I had to be dragged, by the exhaustion of my formalist sensibilities, by the denuding of my cleverness and knack, by failed marriages, by a

too-long sequence of empty rooms filled with shouting instead of sounds, across the threshold of my
competence and authority, all the way into a bar
where someone else was mixing the drinks and somebody else would schedule and drive the trains. In the
Pennsylvania Station, my eyes escaped from me, "finding shelter" in transit. They found a woman singing
before ever I was born. They found a crowd moving
toward destinations unknown. Eyesight, in its purity,
has no precedent and envisions no aftermath. Its everlasting *now* enjoys time as a medium, not as a measure.
"Time is but the stream I go a-fishing in." The opening
stanza of "The Northeast Corridor" resists this *now*
until it can resist no longer. Its "last line of defense"
proves to be, like all such lines—Maginot, Siegfried,
etc.—a fantasy of secured imperatives, a wishful thinking. The poem begins, when it properly begins, at the
end of questions. (To the list above—Traherne, Blake,
Ronald Johnson—I ought of course to have added Saint
Henry. As he wrote in *Walden:* "I awoke to an answered
question.") The eye that sees without a doubt, without
interrogation and uninterrupted by comparisons, continues to see. It is awash (Henry's stream is a stream,
not a metaphor) in the delightful fluid participle: living, not life. "Without the politics" of sad affiliation to
an abdicated I, the eye can swarm with the crowd, can
sing with the dead. In this sense, then, the purpose of

all poems is disaffiliation—that great divorcing command all over again.

But as for me, I had to be dragged. A fugitive makes a reluctant commuter, impatient with waiting and all too vigilant to enjoy the things and people that he sees. Escape is an outcome but not a means of ecstasy. In "The Northeast Corridor" ecstasy is driven, like grace abounding even unto the worst of sinners, to dismember me. The poem ends:

> The world is insatiable. It takes your legs off,
> it takes your arms and parades in front of you
> such wonderful things, such pictures of warm houses
> trellised along the sides with green so deep
> it is like black air, only transparent,
> of women singing, of trains of lithium
> on the awakening body of a landscape
> or across the backdrop of an old city
> steaming and high-shouldered as the nineteen-forties.
> The world exhausts everything except my eyes
> because it is a long walk to the world
> begun before I was born. In the far corner
> the dead woman bows off stage. The television
> crumples into a white dot as the last
> train of the evening, my train, is announced.
> I lived in one place. I want to die in another.

This is the use of dismemberment: for liberation. The world's insatiability for identities and intentions complements the eye's insatiability for light, and each is a guarantor or providence. The world consumes us along with itself in headlong, loving apocalypse, without a pause for accounting. (One time he was right, John Berryman, though I don't think he enjoyed it: "Nobody is ever missing.") The eye gorges itself on light until even blackness is not blindness but a sweet transparency.

Ecstasy proves the virtues of helplessness. One of my favorite euphemisms is "legless," meaning drunk. Writing "The Northeast Corridor," I found that my life had gorged on me, and yet I was the drunken one, the legless one. And in that state I found the world's insatiability to be unaccountably generous, a wild providence. Ecstasy is a topsy-turvy, empowering the helplessness upon which it depends and thrives. And so in the Pennsylvania Station I was suddenly shown a splendid display of "wonderful things," and the first of these were "pictures of warm houses"—to my mind, pictures by Édouard Vuillard, my favorite painter and, as I was overjoyed to learn at a party only a week ago, John Ashbery's favorite too. I mean, the way that Vuillard can warm every exterior and thereby transform it to an inside, a loving, domestic space, without in any way compromising its endlessness: *that* is ecstasy in all its quiet topsy-turvy. I was shown transparency, the unresisting site of light's infinite transgression; every blessed thing in this world is a threshold crossed and recrossed effortlessly all the time, even by itself. Who needs legs when he has eyes? And wasn't Julius Caesar a bit of a twit to make such a big deal about the Rubicon? Transparency is a condition of both space and time, of landscapes and of decades. Helplessness travels easily through them all. Only efforts are obstacles, and I was given to write this poem just when my efforts were exhausted. I saw at last when I wasn't looking, and my travels, my "long walk to the world," began "before I was born." When Charles Ives said that "American music is already written," he meant that composers come in the middle; music passes through them along its way. Poetry passes through us. Nobody lives in the Pennsylvania Station, though everyone passing through is alive at the time. In "The Northeast Corridor" I began to see that "I" in poems is a transparent eyeball, the better to see *through* with, my dears. (Insert here your own fondest memory of Ralph Waldo Emerson's *Nature.*) In the Iron Horse bar, I was not the man who left Wisconsin. As I drank the whiskey John Cheever poured for me, I was not the man who would knock at my sister's door that night. An I does not depart. An I does not arrive. I is a transparent membrane crossing over only as it is crossed through. Thus is transparency a velocity and helplessness ecstasy. It was in "The Northeast Corridor" and, indeed, all through my *New Dark Ages* that I came to realize the great help of Arthur Rimbaud, especially as it is so beautifully offered up in his famous letter of May 13, 1871, to Georges Izambard:

> I'm degrading myself as much as possible now. Why? I want to be a poet, and I'm working to turn myself into a *seer;* you don't understand at all and I don't know how to explain it. It's all a matter of arriving at the unknown via the derangement of *all the senses.* . . . This is not my fault at all. It's wrong to say: I think. Better to say: Someone thinks me. Pardon the word-game. I is an other. Too bad for the wood that finds it is a violin. . . .

> *[translation mine]*

Rimbaud says "dérangement," and I say "dismemberment." Rimbaud says "violin," and I say "television." Let's call the whole thing off. What happens is that a poet sees by degrading the I. So doing, he exalts the eye set free from its false sovereign, Self. A deranged eye sees fine. The light enters it effortlessly and unimpeded. The optic nerves speed the news. Only the

I feels lost, feels frightened, deprived of its unfair interpretive advantage. But the poet is *not* I. He's gone on. He's an other. He's sped with the news, boarded the light-speed express—in my recalcitrant case, "the last train of the evening." I embraced the Gospel according to Rimbaud in early middle age, not a moment too soon. God knows how many septinas I might otherwise have made. "The Northeast Corridor" ends with a wish that is instantly a wish no more. Being alive, one has no choice but to die as one lives, i.e., elsewhere. Write it. Necessity sets us free from wishes. Light carries us away.

To join the crowd at the slam, to lust openly . . .

The line above appears in Ann Lauterbach's "Boy Sleeping," the poem that has been murmuring to me, more tenderly than I can say, while I wrote my pages about "The Northeast Corridor." I must tell you. Sometimes there is one particular poem that comes along and exponentially changes the possibilities of writing within a given life: in this case, mine. I was midway through the making of New Dark Ages, *and I was well and truly clueless as to how to proceed. I'd garnered a good sense of my exhaustion. I was at home with helplessness. But damned if any ecstasy was showing through. And then the mail came. (I had a wonderful mailman in those days, a young black man with terrible feet. Sometimes he would dodge the postal inspectors who seemed always to hound him and spend half an hour or so in my kitchen with his shoes off, sharing my soup.) Among the bills and circulars was the brand-new issue of* Pequod, *the magazine edited so courageously lo these many years by poet Mark Rudman. The magazine contained an essay of mine about Joseph Cornell as well as two poems from the stalled, unfinished* New Dark Ages. *Like poets everywhere, I turned immediately to my own work, read it through, and then . . . on the next page after my little cluster of pages, there it was for the first time: "Boy Sleeping." It begins this way:*

These difficulties—flamboyant tide, modest red
   berries,
or modest tide, flamboyant berries—
the moon keeping and casting light
onto the boy's sleeping face
and the posture of his knowledge
erected on the fatal—

                     Is this how it begins?
Or is the solid figure of the night
only a wish to survive the last word said
so that such natural things induce furthering
after the episode of the shut.

Should I tell him his face mirrors the lost?
Should I tell him to wake, marry, find, escape

The one whose voice exhausts itself on the recurrent
whose fraudulence speaks without images
whose desire spends itself
on indifference, and whose light
makes light of us, those of us whose bearing is
to continue—

                What is the sublime
but a way, under the pressure of not knowing but
    caring,
to join the crowd at the slam, to lust openly . . .

Nothing before and nothing since ever sounded so true so fast. I was sped. Having spent the first part of my writing life opposing shape to change, fending off rescue with recalcitrance, virtue with stubbornness, how wonderful to find that shape and change, berries and tides, are one and the same, ecstatically, interchangeable! How good to find a wish surviving at the end of necessity, the wish to wordlessness that is the life of poetry beyond all poems! How warm to find in the nature of all "natural things" a ready means of escape! Closure is an episode. You sleepwalk out of it, easy as that. Or by loving the sleep in all things, or in anything, you waken from a dream of vigilance to the helpless ecstasy of love. Lauterbach shows it all in its proper sequence: "wake, marry, find, escape." I open my eyes. Instantly, I am married by light to the world and carried away. Easy as that. And so exhaustion proves to be the very threshold of waking, not its antipode. Crossing over, the exhausted voice is spoken for: "I is an other." Crossing over, the exhausted eye is enlightened: "Who made the eyes but I?" Sublimity is the way of light and the way by which the light makes lights of us. We are sped. I walked out of the Iron Horse at last to join the crowd and the trains, thanks, in such bedazzled retrospect, to Ann.

And so I meant to be a legless walker and a see-through ecstatic. But as I think you know, I have always been a very slow learner, and so, as I began to write the poems in my fourth collection, I carried still a significant burden of ghost-pain and opacity. My book *Erasures* therefore, unsurprisingly, proved to be a kind of clean-up operation, a little "climbing/before the take-off," to borrow yet again a parcel of words from Ezra Pound. I've always loved erasers. One of my favorite chores in grade school was to carry the board erasers down into the basement where there was a great machine that sucked them black and clean again. One of my favorite cartoons has always been the one in which Bugs Bunny seizes the artist's pencil and then erases hapless Daffy Duck again and again. And among the living American painters, my favorite is surely Robert Rauschenberg. I never tire of the example of one early practice: his erasing of a drawing by de Kooning, whom he loved.

> And then Rauschenberg, hemming and hawing, asked the older man if he might have a drawing. That in itself was not unusual. Artist friends often exchanged work. But Rauschenberg wanted the drawing not to hang in his studio, but to *erase.*
>
> *(from* De Kooning: An American Master
> *by Mark Stevens and Annalyn Swan)*

But there's a difference, obviously. In my own experience and practice, I myself was the all-too-beloved forebear I needed to erase. It was my own facility that needed irreversible undoing. I wanted words that spoke for white space and a way with words that opened ways on the pages just as a transparent teardrop opens and prepares afresh an eye to see. Prose was a way, and in many of the poems in *Erasures* blocks of unrelated, paratactic prose regularly interrupt the free-verse lyric motion, making, if not mayhem, at least a little quiet for a while. For example, in "A Type of Agnes:"

Where it was raining
he built a bicycle underneath the cars,
silvered. I needed
desperately to return
to be lovers.
Beautiful house in shade,
who never returned
I never knew.

We must kill the street because it brings too many
    people forward into
light they cannot bear, into the accusations they
    cannot answer. If
Heaven takes an animal by the throat, it is a torch.
    Seized by dissent,
it invents the traffic. The selfless lesbian Geschwitz
    in the adagio.

The self-referent I is interrupted in its plangent gestur-
ing by spastic gestures in the prose. Okay. But interruption has a ways to go before it constitutes erasure.
And a spasm isn't ecstasy, however often the two are
confused in our degraded day. I needed to turn my eyes
inside out and to use them cleanly. I needed to exteri-
orize inwardness like the wound it was. I went looking
for a new page fresh for poems.

It happened in Missouri, where I had gone to be a visiting professor, a poetry faculty of One for one entire year. (Displacement is a ready-made means of erasure. Sometimes the best thing you can do for your poems is to go where nobody knows you, and where nothing in sight or sound chimes with a single blessed thing inside you. Forget about the writers' colony. Go to the mountains of the moon and pay attention.) It happened in another big, big house. I did my reading and writing in a sunny room upstairs. (Never forget what W. H. Auden said: "only the Devil writes at night.") And it was a pleasure to look up from my book and down to where the numberless next-door children would be playing. One in particular, a radiantly fearless little girl, was given to walking right up to my window on home-made stilts. How do you go about erasing yourself, how dispose of such a perilous and long-beloved forebear? Look up. Look out. Eyesight is erasure widening the eyebeam's way. The Ancient Mariner knew. The loving eye overwhelms poor, sad awareness, and freedom (freedom is love) floods in from the outside.

> Oh happy living things! no tongue
> Their beauty might declare:
> A spring of love gushed from my heart,
> And I blessed them unaware:

Sure my kind saint took pity on me,
And I blessed them unaware.

*(from "The Rime of the Ancient Mariner,"
Samuel Taylor Coleridge)*

Instead of water snakes, numberless children thronged
my driveway. My saint was a kid on stilts.

We are living in the beautiful district.
The wind lets no leaf touch the ground.
Next door, in bright sun, a girl on stilts
is so fabulously illuminated
she blends into the light below her legs.

(from "Heat Lightning")

Spontaneous, gratuitous affirmation makes off with
mind, with motive and awareness. What did Rauschenberg contribute to de Kooning? His absence. How did
the Ancient Mariner save himself? By being saved, by
hapless overwhelming love. The girl on stilts strode
forth to me out of heaven, which is daylight, and in the
unschematic erasure of my self-awareness, she was indistinguishable from that light: "she blends into the light
below her legs." Where there is no telling the difference,
there is no difference. If I is an other, who is there to
tell? We are already all of us gone into the world of light,

so why not go? Distinctions only exacerbate apartness, only originate in a solitary mind keeping its poor, sad distances from heaven. I used to think that poetry was a way of telling one thing from another and that, writing it, I might arrange the differences my way: the dream of syntax; the miserable labor camp of subject, verb, and object; the poem as autistic puzzle; the poet as drunken nostalgiac in the Iron Horse Bar. There are no differences. Light and each and every thing illuminated strides on stilts at 186,000 miles per second (the speed limit in Missouri, as I recall), right through the windows of the soul, your soul and my soul, into a poem and out again. Erasure means the end of interiors. Where's poetry? Where the eye's turned inside out.

In "Heat Lightning" I was given to begin to use the wisdom in chapter 9 of the Gospel of St. Mark:

> And if thine eye offend thee, pluck it out: it is
> better for thee to enter into the kingdom of God
> with one eye, than having two eyes to be cast into
> hell fire . . .

(St. Mark 9:47)

My own hell fire had been a formalist's defilement of change and a self-willed isolation from the heavenly kingdom of change, which is daylight. (With so many stars shining down through our galaxy, it must always be daylight where we see.) Spontaneous, gratuitous affirmation comes easily to one who sees the children in his driveway borne aloft by light, who, by simply looking up, is given to see what Ezra Pound saw when he saw "the child/walk in peace in her basilica,/The light there almost solid . . ."

> Concede a limb to save a limb, an eye
> for an eye that looks outward only.
> My heart was a sieve of law and had
> no reward but another child's slower illness
> on the ward where they made Christmas in July
> and every month. The stockings never came down.

> On the old street, sacrifice depended
> upon faith. In the beautiful district,
> light stands firm beneath the children,
> I live alone, undiscarded, and
> sacrifice is the ordinary of each day.
> Sun and wind intensify
> without interruption and we blend
> to one color the color of windows.

With an eye for outward only, I was no longer the Pharisee of myself, "a sieve of law." With an eye for outward only, I could see a daily Christmas come *and* go, showing the children strong and well as it went. With an eye for outward, I could see the abandonment of myself to change as the routine and delightful sacrifice of darkness (which never has existed in the outside world) unto daylight. And such sacrifice does not require an act of faith but, rather, transpires in the beautiful, everlasting prelude to it, i.e., in mere existence. Poems happen not because of faith, but just before. And so a poetics need never be doctrinal. Whatever it is I believe, I shall wait and see. In the meanwhile, I can see the neighbors' children striding on stilts of light. I can see the day's splendid display of wind strengthening and sun strengthening (sun and wind are healthy children too) "without interruption," because an eye for outward only neither strays nor suffers pause. I've said there are no differences. Light is all the colors shining as one where the windows are clean, and the transparent eyeball shares that color too.

Beginning my fifth collection I felt, for me, an unprecedented confidence in the world's work and in poetry's lucent, uninterrupted part in it all. For the first time in a very long time, writing felt to be a perfect happiness, the easy acknowledgment of a providence I did not need to cajole. Titling the book was one such acknowledgment, an early thanks for the permission Ann

Lauterbach, in "Boy Sleeping," had given to my poems. In New York one evening, after a poetry reading, my wife Claudia and I went out to dinner with Ann. We had a lovely time, and during the cab ride afterwards I told her how much I liked the beautiful, grass-green blouse that she was wearing. A few days later, when we got home to Colorado, Claudia and I found a package waiting on the steps. It was from Ann, and inside was the grass-green blouse. Providence outsped us home. I called my fifth collection *Beautiful Shirt,* and it remains to this day my favorite of all my books. Not necessarily my best—a paucity of reviews and poor sales may well attest to *that*—it is, however, the one I most enjoy the memory of writing because I scarcely remember writing it at all. One of the epigraphs of this little book comes from *Walden:* "In Arcadia, when I was there, I did not see any hammering stone." *Beautiful Shirt* entailed no hammering, no work at all. ("And you can say *that* again," I seem to hear some critic exclaiming still.) The poems came in packets of sunlight through the window from the garden. They came in parcels of grass-green garments from my friends.

The opening poem is one such garden piece, exemplary, if for no other reason, because its flowers and personae wholly occupy preludial moments in which words wait for the poetry they'll believe. Not still, the waiting is busy with attention. And this busyness is one other way in which "Lyre" exemplifies my happiness in *Beautiful Shirt:* I'd finally come round from the enchantments of Orphism and from the imagination of poems that mean to bind the world with spells. I'd recovered from Rilke. I did not wish, as he does in the first of *The Sonnets to Orpheus,* to still the "creatures of stillness" with my song. Rather, I listened to hear them filling it with new sounds, their sounds, spoken from everlasting, before and afterwards.

> Before anything could happen,
> flecks of real gold
> on her mouth, her eyes more
> convex than any others,
> the ground spoke, the barrier
> of lilacs spoke. What sang
> in the black tree was entirely gold.
> Her chair was empty.
>
> New absence is a great fugue
> dark as the underskin of fruit.
> At the center of the earth
> it surrounds and amplifies the dead
> whose music never slows down.

Happy to find myself writing free verse carelessly at last (even the mischief of *Erasures* was a kind of espionage, a "pentameter by other means"), I'd found gold without a moment's prospecting, right there on the surfaces everywhere available: lips and eyes, lilacs and the singing tree. Of course, I gave a thought to John Berryman, a good man afflicted by Orphism all his life. Remember the first of *The Dream Songs?* "Once in a sycamore I was glad / all at the top, and I sang." He shouldn't have. Imagine the rescue he might have heard in the singing of the tree! But I didn't think of Berryman too long. Gold is gold, and the insistence of everything about lilacs, sight and sound (it is for their insistence that we love them, and *at* their insistence, I do believe, that summer ever comes to our cold climates), defies distraction. The world is the occasion prior to all occasions, and their sole survivor too. Listening, I heard as much, and it was a treasure to me. Attention empties the chairs, and the emptiness is filled with garden states. And in seeing convex eyes, I saw that my own garden's state, given over to free verse carelessly, would not only amplify itself (convexity spreads all surface wide) but deepen without ever suffering the sad paralysis of depth. (I think that's why they put Hell down below us, the ancients, sensing depth to be commensurate with sure damnation.) All the arguments I've ever heard about aesthetics come down to an unnecessary antagonism between the superficial and the deep, the surface meaning and the deeper meaning meant to make a shadow or a fool of surfaces. Look at a garden. The surfaces are delightful, and there are depths everywhere, spreading those surfaces into a greeny further dream, which is entirely true and which is a surface too. Eyes *are* convex. To see is to spread, though Orpheus doesn't want us to believe it. He needs there to be a King in Hell for his singing to oppose. He needs the entirely hallucinatory antagonism between surfaces and depth to make his mission to Eurydice matter. The throne of Hell is empty. Hell is empty. Every open eye, every syllable spoken by the lilacs, proves that this is so. Disposing of Orpheus voids the antagonism. And in that void, writing "Lyre," I heard an amplification of surfaces at the surface and underneath it, too. Beneath the skin of a fruit is an underskin. Depth never stills the spreading, and Eurydice is safe and sovereign everywhere she goes. (I could, at this point, go off on a tear about the ways in which depth has been misused to abject the feminine in us all, but I wouldn't have much fun, and others have expressed it infinitely better than I could. Reread *Tender Buttons* or Barbara Guest's *Fair Realism.* Revisit the paintings of Joan Mitchell. Blow a raspberry at Orpheus. You'll find, as I did, that very soon it amplifies itself into a fugue.) The uprooting of depth, its liberation if you like, is no deprivation. Convexity is not distortion. Apples have cores, but the cores are seeds, not stones. They incline to going on, to the amplification of apples. The core is a surface spreading, too. Everything's central. In this regard, I am always glad to remember an early passage from

Ashbery's inexhaustible meditation on Parmigianino's masterpiece, "Self-Portrait in a Convex Mirror:"

> . . . The whole is stable within
> Instability, a globe like ours, resting
> On a pedestal of vacuum, a ping-pong ball
> Secure on its jet of water.
> And just as there are no words for the surface, that is,
> No words to say what it really is, that it is not
> Superficial but a visible core, then there is
> No way out of the problem of pathos vs. experience.
> You will stay on, restive, and serene in
> Your gesture which is neither embrace nor warning
> But which holds something of both in pure
> Affirmation that doesn't affirm anything.

More antagonisms and antinomies disappear in these few lines than Orpheus could ever shake a plectrum at. We take our pathos with us where we go, and the bottom of the garden is not a hell but another green place. Centers do not solve, but, rather, amplify the mysteries of all surfaces, which amplify the centers in their turn. Our Earth, floating in space, is mysterious, but there it is, no more puzzling than is a ping-pong ball upon its jet of water. Our words can never say the mystery of our meanings, but there they are: spoken and meaning worlds to us. (Otherwise why am I writing, why are you reading this?) Under the aegis of our effortless at-tentions, the restive serenity John Ashbery describes (writing poetry is a restive serenity, isn't it? kind of like playing center field on a balmy summer day when a big-name batter's up) not only *is* pure, but, more im-portantly, remains pure, whatever comes. Eurydice was never in any danger. Mysterious but not puzzling, her purity is the plain speech I heard in the lilacs. Her dis-appearance, like theirs, does not confuse the issue of her perfection, affirming nothing that goes unsaid. In absence I also heard an amplification not even death it-self delays. Death isn't delay; like everything, it makes a sound to anyone who's listening, and listening contin-ues sounds, just as seeing speeds the light along. Con-tinuity, I found, is amplification. Take it easy, Orpheus. Winter never delayed a lilac by a single day.

I ended "Lyre" beside myself with the happiness of just such a certainty. Prelude and aftermath kissed me, each on one eye. And the kisses amplified everything well beyond the scope of any imagination, most especially mine.

Imagination did not make the world.

Sweetness is the entire portion.
Before anything could happen,

happiness, the necessary
precondition of the world,
spoke and flowered over the hill.

When I was in Hell
on the ruined palisade,
either mystery or loneliness
kissed my open eyes.
It felt hugely convex, seeing
and immediately forgetting.

By contrast, what I imagined
later was nothing.

In the garden, I had fallen upon independence, the
way that Marvell fell upon grass, i.e., gratefully: independence from the imagination that life is a puzzle
to be solved; from the imagination of perils where
none exists; from the imagination of the imagination
itself, that self-enchantment that pretends to animate
a universe already entirely alive in each and every
vivid particular. *Felix culpa,* yes indeed. Marvell's gardener exclaimed "What wondrous life is this I lead!"
and I concurred: "Sweetness is the entire portion."
Which is to say also that every portion is, in its sweetness, an entirety. Nothing's ever missing. Eurydice
isn't gone, nor do the lilacs ever stop speaking. I know

it must seem almost ludicrous to be making an argument on behalf of happiness; I mean, who's against it? Well, as it turns out, almost every anthology is full of antagonists, latter-day Orphics whose authority depends upon mischance and repair. (They're like those crooked mechanics who squirt oil underneath your perfect car and tell you that you're leaking oil and need them and their pricey expertise.) I hold this truth to be self-evident when I am in my senses: the world is happy to be here. The only question, then: am I? The open eye is glad the light preceded it. The listener thrills to hear the already eloquent, irrefutable babble of this world. Where the influence is real, there is no anxiety. Why worry about Wordsworth so long as there are daffodils? What problem is Milton when the trees are clearly overflowing still with Edens? The imagination is Oedipal (I know I'm mixing myths as mischievously as I mix metaphors, but those are the breaks), thinking to enjoy the favors of the world by destroying its predecessor, which is the world itself. Orpheus, you poor booby, I've been to Hell and it was already a ruin, haunted by nobody but you and your ephebes from the anthologies. And then the minute I opened my eyes it was gone, abolished by kisses which, as predecessors go, get sweeter all the time. As Ashbery writes in his very newest book (as of today, that is, June 7, 2005), *Where Shall I Wander?:*

Nobody believes in heaven. Hell is what gets them
    fired up.
I'm probably the only American

who thinks he's going to heaven, though my reasons
would be hard to explain. I enjoy seasons
and picnicking. A waft from a tree branch
and I'm in heaven . . .

(from "Novelty Love Trot")

Eyesight amplifies the convexity of the eye, and the world widens. The imagination is late to the event, receding to a pinpoint (Orpheus himself is the hapless bride of Hades) as its happy predecessor descries Edens unforeseen.

It's getting late, and our conversation comes in sight of its end. It feels more important than ever, then, to be neither flippant nor glib, but, rather, to be cautious in my carelessness and, also, clear. I want to be helpful, and so it's wise to acknowledge and detail my helps. I know that I've been pretty rough on Orpheus, playing fast and loose with one who is, after all, an abiding presence and potency. Two of the sharpest texts in my revisionary life—William Carlos Williams's Kora in Hell *and Denise Levertov's "A Tree Telling of Orpheus"—would, after all, have been impossible without him. And there is a third text, sharper still to me and more instructive. In* Prolegomena *to the Study of Greek Religion, Jane Ellen Harrison accomplishes, among almost innumerable wonders, the restoration of Orpheus to his fullest and most human place in actual events. She brings him very near, and it is because of that nearness that I have been able to make and to hone my own determinations concerning his role and influence in my poetics of attention. Here's one passage that woke and emboldened me:*

> In Pompeian wall-paintings and Graeco-Roman sarcophagi it is as magical musician, with power over all wild untamed things in nature, that Orpheus appears. This conception naturally passed into Christian art and it is interesting to watch the magical musician transformed gradually into the Good Shepherd. The bad wild beasts, the lions and lynxes, are weeded out one by one, and we are left, as in the wonderful Ravenna mosaic, with only a congregation of mild patient sheep.

Harrison, by force of simplest but most thorough attention *articulates my gripe with Orpheus to me. I cannot think of poetry, and I do not* want *to think of it, as a power over anything, most especially the wild. Rather, I have found poetry to be the soul of wildness itself,*

*an energy that delivers me, grateful and helpless, all
the way over to where the wild things thrive. I worship
Christ because he throws me to the lions who love me.
I write poems to show I love the lions too. One way to
think about this book that I've been writing is as a re-
jection or, God willing, as a refutation of any practice
that finds badness in wildness or seeks power over the
sovereign powers of this world. Reader, I never think of
you as mild.*

> Lion that eats my mind now for a decade knowing
>   only your hunger
> Not the bliss of your satisfaction O roar of the
>   Universe how am I chosen
> In this life I have heard your promise I am ready to
>   die I have served
> Your starved and ancient Presence O Lord I wait in
>   my room at your Mercy.

> *(from "The Lion for Real," Allen Ginsberg)*

*And there is one more passage from Harrison's master-
work in which her attention to Orpheus rises far above
argument, all the way into an empyrean of good use.*

> Once we are fairly awake to the fact that Orpheus
> was a real live man, not a faded god, we are struck
> by the human touches in his story, and most by a

certain vividness of emotion, a reality and personality of like and dislike that attends him. . . . Always
about him there is this aloof air, this remoteness,
not only of the self-sufficing artist, who is and must
be always alone, but of the scrupulous moralist and
reformer . . . who . . . draws men and repels them,
not by persuading their reason, still less by enflaming
their passions, but by sheer magic of his personality.

*I love Jane Ellen Harrison for using that most wonderful
of words,* awake. *And here again she wakens me to the
particulars and substance of my* dislike *for Orpheus,
my fellow man. Myself, I read and write for nearness,
not remoteness. I know that I'm alone, and yet I always hope for grace to say, as Robert Creeley said,* "I
am still alone, but want you with me." *Even in prayer,
I mean to be alone* with *the Alone. Most important of
all, I teach and write to act on the belief that poetry's
magic* ("Nothing's more real than magic"—Malcolm
Lowry) *is nothing to do with personality, but is, instead,
a continuing instance of the eye's objective immortality. My eyes owe much to the wild insight of Jane Ellen
Harrison.*

Happiness is, among so many things, the freedom to
take one's own advice. And when I had the happiness,
thanks to a sabbatical and the windfall of a fellowship,
to take a year away from teaching, I took a year away

from home and from the ordinary use of my language. My money would not stretch as far as the mountains of the moon, but it got us to the Netherlands for a good while, and then to a small, small town near Clermont, in southern France. My hope was to be a stranger. As I'd written in my fellowship application, my hope was to write a poem as nobody at all. I wanted an unaffiliated eye for things and an unschooled ear for any sound they made. It was a fine year, and I was given to write the poems of my next book, *There Are Three*, by attentions I was more or less compelled to pay to everything unrecognizable in those fine days. (I'd taken the precaution of sending a box of books ahead to France, but it never arrived, thank God. And so the only English-on-paper we had near Clermont were: a poem of Robert Creeley's tucked inside my wallet; an old Penguin edition of *Great Expectations* loaned to us by a sympathetic expatriate living in a village down the road; and, bizarrely, a British lingerie catalog that a shy young neighbor brought to the door one day, hoping we could translate the order forms into French for him. It was plenty.) Where communication is out of the question and self-expression might as well whistle down the wind, language keeps close, close company with the eye, rampant with it and entirely in its charge. I was a new child to myself, playing at poetry, and play, like creation, is change for the sake of change alone.

One morning I was playing with the word (I'd heard it over the little kitchen radio) "bourgeois." After a while, I laughed to see two other words inside of it—"bois rouge"—and then I started writing the first poem of my vacation book.

> The red forest is
> eager to be seen.
> The red fragrance
> travels a great distance,
> meaning nothing in
> general, but in
> particular fatal
> and entirely personal.
>
> The soul at present
> matters less than
> instinct, its
> later instrument . . .

> *(from "A Branch of the Discipline")*

These lines were carelessly free in a brand-new way to me. Having got out of the habit, outside, of using English sensibly, I used it sensually, for the sake of the game I was playing. "Bois rouge" was my red forest, and why should not a senseless forest be colored

red? It had presented itself by stepping out of "bour-geois," and there wasn't any reason in the world *not* to welcome such a willing, such an "eager" anomaly. It made the game by making a world in which to play it. Creation is change for the sake of change alone. (God's plan is not to have a Plan; that's how human freedom can shake hands with the doctrine of predestination. God's a good role model. Ask Jack Spicer: "Poet be like God.") And when change *is* alone, unencumbered by the communicative wiles and expressive whims of one-self and one's intentions, it goes wild. It shows in the line breaks; having nobody to please, they please them-selves; and pleasing themselves, they are a pleasure, pure and simple. "Fragrance" rhymes with "distance" so easily when no one's counting. Sense travels fast where no meanings intervene. Generality and particularity fold their tents and forget their differences. Forgetting may be fatal, but fatal only to priority. Self is safely, happily ahead of the game, being in the game, and has no care to take things personally. As William Blake avowed, annihilation is the Heaven selfhood seeks by seeing through, and not with, the eye. And what's to fear? Annihilation is a furthering, a "later instru-ment." In my fellowship application, I'd also set myself the task of proving the nonexistence of the soul. Some-times, error is the saving of a man.

> The red forest maintains
> perfect silence, eager
> to be seen without
> distraction. In clear
> heavens of destruction
> it aborts the unspoken
> words so easy to defy.
> The soul is a nest.

In *There Are Three,* although I had not planned it, I for once became the experimental writer some folks already, for good or ill, believed me to be. Experiment has nothing to do with obscurity, and neither is it bent upon proving that language is a hoax or heaven a canard. Meaning to show the soul up for the wishful, willful thinking I presumed it to be, I stumbled into a nest, and out again, through an undistracted eye. Vision annihilates point of view. Sight abandons the nest. In poetry, the unspoken is better left alone so as to see what's next to say. The unspoken is backward. Its notion of the soul is something like a bowl of soup that one must somehow carry through life, hoping against hope to spill as little as humanly possible until death. But experiment must never look backward. It loves clarity, and it is eager, like a fledgling eye, to see its way clear to the next heaven and then to the heaven after that. In the perfection of silence—"bois rouge" silenced "bourgeois" one morning in France when I was playing—poetry rings true. That wonderful man Gerrard Winstanley, founder of my favorite seventeenth-century utopian society, the Diggers, found grace to declare that "The Truth is always Experimentall [*sic?* I don't think so]." And that explains my quibble with so much of what passes for experimental writing now. If one's purpose is a naysaying (e.g., the error of my fellowship proposal), if one's purport is to expose the mendacity of one's medium and thus to loose a relativist chimera upon the objective immortality of absolutely everything, where's Truth? No Truth, no experiment. The empty nest proves that birds can fly; it's a great experiment. I only wish that I had brought one to the science fair when I was a schoolboy. Irony and speculation are always reactionary, never avant-garde. Avant-garde is a bird in flight. It proves itself momently and silently out of words in the empty air, like prayer.

> The soul catches the wind
> between numerals. Once
> I was eager to remain outside
> forever, and once I did.
> The future bent
> the boughs to breaking.

They cracked silently,
one last thing.

Soul escapes upon the wind of things, becoming real,
becoming numberless. Poetry exteriorizes our words: a
sight for sore eyes. They are not empty; they are broken
open by their futures now. (There are many futures. One
"forever" has nothing to do with another, but is eternal,
like all of them.) When the bough breaks, the poem will
fall, but up mounts the poetry, experiment-all.

                    . . . It goes fast.

Scramble it, make an omelet
out of it, for the hell of it . . .

                    (from "Oh Max," Robert Creeley)

It certainly does go fast, and then faster. Velocities, I
think, are what prove our poems true. They are the as-
piration of words approaching light-speed, eager to be
seen, as I saw in the red forest. At play (play is what
I'd been missing with my all-too-earnest eyes) in *There
Are Three,* I stumbled into a nest—my soul—and out
again. There I found myself to be the poet I am, stopping
with you here just a little while longer. For some years
now, I've seen my poems on the air. And when I'm well,

when I come to my senses, my none-too-earnest eyes
will speed me to them. This is my testimonial to myself: writing's easy. And while writing my seventh book,
Arcady (what else could I have called it?), ease became
an energy (what else could Walt have meant by the in-
vocation "I loaf and invite my soul?"), something the
old revivalists might have called "a leading." But me, I'd
just as soon call it happiness and say that I am always
happy writing poems. Tolstoy was wise about a lot of
things; but of happiness, he hadn't a clue. Remember
the beginning of *Anna Karenina?*—"Happy families are
all alike; every unhappy family is unhappy in its own
way." I am drawn to the poems I write by their distinctions in the sunlight or against the blue of the sky, just
as surely as I am drawn to the absolute uniqueness of a
petal's edge. Happiness begins in difference, in a sudden change, and continues just so long as the change
is welcome and, I suppose, welcoming. Difference is
not a quarrel. A poem is not a quarrel. Does that make
poetry—families, for that matter, Leo—dull? I'm not
looking for a fight.

One morning I was walking to work along a back alley,
not looking for anything. Then there they were—tiger
lilies all over the place where none had been the day
before. The morning sunlight was all over them. The
flowers had no quarrel with that. Neither did my eyes

or I. One of the better angels of my life suggested
I write it down, and I did. We all went on together a
ways, one happy family sure enough.

Light lily lily light light lily light

Imagically
Lightli ly

Outline stones for the wind

All creatures come
To mind to oneness

Light first and last, and lilies and lights along the way.
The alleyway, in *just* that way and *just* that order, plea-
sured my eyes. Of course it was a happiness to say.
"Only the lull I like" wrote Whitman. If I can see it, it
must be moving; and when I see it, I am moving too.
The lull is not a pause. The lull is an ensemble underway, and as I found, anything I might say would
be an adverb. And so it was—"Imagically/Lightli ly."
Nothing is more real than magic. We modify our motion magically in this world by moving with it, and our
image-making attention is an adverb changing us. See?
Solidity, that stony old soul, escapes upon the wind of
things. Call it the "liquefaction" of the soul. . . . Robert

Herrick would like that, and, foregrounding the letter "l," it pleases me too, like lilies in an alleyway. Light calls. All creatures come. And, next, almost immediately, a new mind comes, making one big soul, a happy family.

I know that happiness does not dispense with sorrow. I began *Arcady* as a memorial to my dear sister who died quite suddenly the night of my son's very first birthday. But although they cannot dispense with pain, the attentions I commend do, I swear it, dispose my eyes and direct my soul to something faster than pain and to places farther than my sorrows go. At the end of *Process and Reality*, Alfred North Whitehead describes this disposition and inclines in the direction of its eventual name: "the whole story."

> The ultimate evil in the temporal world is deeper than any specific evil. It lies in the fact that the past fades, that time is a 'perpetual perishing.' . . . The present fact has not the past fact with it in any full immediacy. The process of time veils the past below distinctive feeling. There is a unison of becoming among things in the present. Why should there not be novelty without loss of this direct unison of immediacy among things? In the temporal world, it is the empirical fact that process entails loss: the past

is present under an abstraction. But there is no reason, of any ultimate metaphysical generality, why this
should be the whole story.

Attentions lift me out of the depths where evils lie,
broadcasting me onto sunshine surfaces where, for example, lilies glow. The broadcast of perpetual perish-
ing is not a sorrow *there*. *There*, the processes of time
luminesce. And luminescence is unison immediately.
In unity, disappearance is not death. It is a brightness
underway—which is to say a *new novelty*. Loss is not
empirical in the world of light, where light and time,
forms and attentions prove to be one and the same.
Take attendance at the speed of light: "Orpheus?"
"Present;" "Eurydice?" "Present." Light is the whole
story, then, past and present. Look over your shoulder
then; you aren't looking backwards anymore. Attention
bears our old friend Heraclitus out: the way up and the
way down, one and the same.

Where I am formless	When I go back into
My breaking through	The ground the deep
Will be far greater	In me whence I came

Light lily lily light light lily light

Imagi
Cally
Lightli
Ly

In the alleyway, my eyes inclined to a present fact, which was lilies all over the place. I was formless there. But breaking through to the lilies, which was no effort, formed a new novelty from me: an entirety, a "whole story" made of lilies made of light. In the alleyway, my past was the ground out of which no lilies glowed the day before. But out of that depth, via the attentions, theirs and mine (souls are heliotropes), new novelty sprang. There is no syntax for such unison; the only words are words—"light lily lily light light lily light," if I do say so myself. Sorrow depends on syntax: e.g., "that was then, this is now." Pain afflicts the parts of speech: *"ou sont les neiges d'antan."* I cannot use "Imagically" in a sentence, but there it is, a union of empirical fact and metaphysical mischief if ever I almost saw one. Nothing is more real than magic when the emphasis falls on every single word. "Lightlily" is an adverb I cannot use to modify anything at all, but there it is, breaking itself apart, assembling flowers I hadn't seen the day before. Once in a red forest, I looked at a word and saw more words than one. It was fun. A few years later, I walked into an alleyway and the sunshine took my words and made new flowers. It was happiness. It goes fast.

The alleyway is a Way, and anymore nowadays I find myself traveling there, fast or slow.

> What you depart from is not the way
> and olive tree blown white in the wind
> washed in the Kiang and Han
> what whiteness will you add to this whiteness,
>
> > what candor?

(from "Canto LXXIV," Ezra Pound)

In just such fashion, I suppose, the soul of George Herbert has never once or never yet risen from the meat and table Love prepared before his eyes. Poetry is happiness, and happiness has no argument to make. "Who made the eyes but I?" The only reply is to go on seeing, feasting one's eyes in the most literal sense of that beautiful expression. "Heaven and Earth begat the perceiver"—"Canto LXXXV." Parented by such powers, we may rest easy in our eyes. "Awareness restful & fake is fatiguing"—"Canto LXXXV." Beyond the lilies, I have no work to do and no argument. As I look back upon my writing life so far, I begin to see it as a zigzag

walk to the world and to see the World as the alleyway
I needed such a long and perplexed time to reach.

> Backward I see in my own days where I sweated
>   through fog
>   with linguists and contenders,
> I have no mockings or arguments, I witness and wait.

(from "Song of Myself")

I end this book with what I pray is, on my part, an end
to contention. Lily means lily, and it is the sound of a
flower, as I see. I see no gaps. I hear no deception in
the sound of a thrush. I wrote my poems to be at home
with words and not, as it turns out, to master or to un-
dermine them. I wrote to reach my being here. Under
the aegis of happiness, my witness has no accusations
anymore to make, content to wait upon a further happiness time will tell. Heaven almost rhymes with "giving
in." But when I look again, Heaven rhymes more perfectly with "given." And that is how I make my poems
now, and for a while now. After *Arcady*, I wrote the
pieces collected in *My Mojave*, and each of them was
given to me, was brought to my attention by a heaven
that gleamed and then became a gleaming in my eyes.
My alleyway gets around.

I remember quite fondly one particular disc jockey—
New York City, 1970s, WPLJ. She would begin her
broadcast every evening saying "Come fly with me now
on the hippest of all trips: the return to reality." Trip's
a great good word, jumbling all together "journey,"
"inclination," "accident," and "way" into something like
a dance: tripping the light fantastic; or, as Milton said
it first of all, "Come and trip it as you go/On the light
fantastic toe." During a few days traveling in the middle
of *My Mojave* I stumbled upon and into an *ars poetica*
now my own, "My Trip." It goes fast and slow—

> I am looking at a smallpox vaccination scar
> In a war movie on the arm
> Of a young actor. He has just swum
> Across a river somewhere in Normandy
> Into the waiting arms of his rejoicing comrades.
>
> Of course, the river's in California,
> And the actor is dead now. Nevertheless,
> This is the first of many hotels this trip,
> And I find myself preferring wars
> To smut on the networks,
> Even as I find myself reading
> *The Pisan Cantos* for the umpteenth time
> Instead of the novel in my bag.

The poet helps me to the question:
Does anything remain of home at home?

Next day is no way of knowing,
And the day after is my favorite,
A small museum really perfect
And a good meal in the middle of it.
As I'm leaving,
I notice a donkey on a vase
Biting the arm of a young girl,
And outside on the steps
A silver fish head glistens beside a bottlecap.
Plenty remains.

The work of poetry is trust,
And under the aegis of trust
Nothing could be more effortless.
Hotels show movies.
Walking around even tired
I find my eyes find
Numberless good things
And my ears hear plenty of words
Offered for nothing over the traffic noise
As sharp as sparrows.

A day and a day, more rivers crossing me.
It really feels that way, I mean

I have changed places with geography,
And rivers and towns pass over me,
Showing their scars, finding their friends.
I like it best when poetry
Gleams or shows its teeth to a girl
Forever at just the right moment.
I think I could turn and live underneath the animals.
I could be a bottlecap.

Going to the airport going home,
I stop with my teacher, now my friend.
He buys me a good breakfast, berries and hotcakes.
We finish and, standing, I hear
One policeman saying to another
Over the newspaper in a yellow booth
"Do you know this word *regret,* Eddie?
What does it mean?"
Plenty of words over the traffic noise,
And nothing could be more effortless.
Catching a glimpse of eternity, even a poor one, says
    it all.

That's all. My questions, even the most pressing and most tender—"Does anything remain of home at home?"—are answered for me almost in advance by things a day and then another bring to my attention. Days are not a way of knowing, and they require no imagining to live. I did not imagine the bottlecap, but I believed it. And then it answered me: "Plenty remains." A godly thing beside the little fish head, it may just as well have said, "Who made the eyes but I?" Belief turns teachers into friends. Believe your eyes. And yes, you heard it right. In eternity, there are no puzzles and no regrets. Poetry glimpses eternity. It happens all the time.

Works Cited

Apollinaire, Guillaume. *Alcools,* trans. Donald Revell.
    Wesleyan University Press, 1995.

———. *The Self-Dismembered Man: Selected Later Poems,*
    trans. Donald Revell. Wesleyan University Press, 2004.

Ashbery, John. *The Mooring of Starting Out.* The Ecco Press,
    1997.

———. *Self-Portrait in a Convex Mirror.* The Viking Press,
    1975.

———. *Where Shall I Wander.* Ecco/HarperCollins, 2005.

Auden, W. H. *Collected Poems.* Random House, 1976.

Beckett, Samuel. *Endgame* and *Act without Words.* Grove
    Press, 1970.

Berryman, John. *The Dream Songs.* Farrar, Straus & Giroux,
    1969.

Blake, William. *Blake's Poetry and Designs,* eds. Mary Lynn
    Johnson & John E. Grant. Norton, 1979.

Cage, John. *Silence.* Wesleyan Univesity Press, 1961.

Coleridge, Samuel Taylor. *Selected Poems,* ed. Richard
    Holmes. HarperCollins, 1996.

Creeley, Robert. *The Collected Poems.* University of
    California Press, 1982.

———. *So There.* New Directions, 1998.

Eigner, Larry. *Selected Poems.* Oyez Press, 1971.

Emerson, Ralph Waldo. *Selected Essays,* ed. Larzer Ziff.
    Penguin Books, 1982.

Ginsberg, Allen. *Collected Poems.* Harper & Row, 1984.

Goethe, Johann Wolfgang von. *Conversations with Eckermann,* trans. John Oxenford. Da Capo, 1998.

Harrison, Jane Ellen. *Prolegomena to the Study of Greek Religion.* Princeton University Press, 1991.

Herbert, George. *The Temple,* ed. Louis L. Martz. Oxford University Press, 1986.

Ives, Charles. *Essays before a Sonata, The Majority, and Other Writings.* Norton, 1961.

Johnson, Ronald. *The Book of the Green Man.* Longmans, 1967.

——. *Ark.* Living Batch Press, 1996.

——. *The Shrubberies.* Flood Editions, 2001.

Lauterbach, Ann. *Clamor.* Viking Penguin, 1991.

Lawrence, D. H. *Selected Letters,* ed. Richard Aldinton. Penguin, 1950.

Levertov, Denise. *Poems 1968-1972.* New Directions, 1987.

——. *This Great Unknowing: Last Poems.* New Directions, 2000.

Olson, Charles. *The Maximus Poems,* ed. George Butterick. University of California Press, 1983.

——. *Archaeologist of Morning.* Grossman Publishers, 1973.

Pound, Ezra. *Personae.* New Directions, 1971.

——. *The Cantos of Ezra Pound.* New Directions, 1970.

Revell, Donald. *From the Abandoned Cities.* Harper & Row, 1983.

——. *The Gaza of Winter.* University of Georgia Press, 1988.

——. *New Dark Ages.* Wesleyan University Press, 1990.

——. *Erasures.* Wesleyan University Press, 1992.

——. *Beautiful Shirt.* Wesleyan University Press, 1994.

——. *There Are Three.* Wesleyan University Press, 1998.

——. *Arcady.* Wesleyan University Press, 2002.

——. *My Mojave.* Alice James Books, 2004.

——. *Pennyweight Windows: New & Selected Poems.* Alice
James Books, 2005.

Rilke, Rainer Maria. *Ahead of All Parting: Selected Poetry
and Prose,* trans. Stephen Mitchell. Random House, 1995.

Rimbaud, Arthur. *Complete Works, Selected Letters,* trans.
Wallace Fowlie. University of Chicago Press, 1966.

——. *A Season in Hell/The Illuminations,* trans. Enid
Peschel. Oxford, 1973.

Shelley, Percy Bysshe. *Complete Poetical Works.* Oxford,
1905.

Spicer, Jack. *The Collected Books,* ed. Robin Blaser. Black
Sparrow Press, 1975.

Stevens, Mark, and Swan, Annalyn. *De Kooning: An
American Master.* Knopf, 2004.

Thoreau, Henry David. *Journal,* eds. John C. Broderick,
Robert Sattelmeyer, Elizabeth Hall Witherall et al. 7 vols.
to date. Princeton University Press, 1981–.

——. *Walden,* ed. J. Lyndon Shanley. Princeton University
Press, 1971.

Traherne, Thomas. *Poems, Centuries, and Three
Thanksgivings,* ed. Anne Ridler. Oxford, 1966.

Virgil. *The Aeneid,* trans. Allen Mandelbaum. Bantam, 1961.

Whitehead, Alfred North. *Process and Reality.* Macmillan,
1929.

Whitman, Walt. *Complete Poetry and Collected Prose,* ed.
Justin Kaplan. Library of America, 1982.

Williams, William Carlos. *The Collected Poems: Volume I, 1909–1939,* eds. A. Walton Litz & Christopher MacGowan. New Directions, 1986.

———. *Paterson.* New Directions, 1963.

Wright, James. *Above the River: The Complete Poems.* The Noonday Press, 1992.

Permission Acknowledgments

DONALD REVELL is the author of ten collections of poetry, including *A Thief of Strings, Pennyweight Windows: New & Selected Poems,* and *My Mojave,* which received the Lenore Marshall Poetry Prize. He is also the author of *Invisible Green: Selected Prose,* a translation of Arthur Rimbaud's *A Season in Hell,* and two translations of Guillaume Apollinaire, *The Self-Disremembered Man* and *Alcools.* Revell is currently poetry editor of *Colorado Review,* and since 1994, he has been a Professor of English at the University of Utah in Salt Lake City. He lives in the desert south of Las Vegas with his wife, poet Claudia Keelan, and their two children.

The text of *The Art of Attention* is set in Warnock Pro, a typeface designed by Robert Slimbach for Adobe Systems in 2000. Book design by Wendy Holdman. Composition by Prism Publishing Center. Manufactured by Bookmobile on acid-free, 30 percent postconsumer wastepaper.